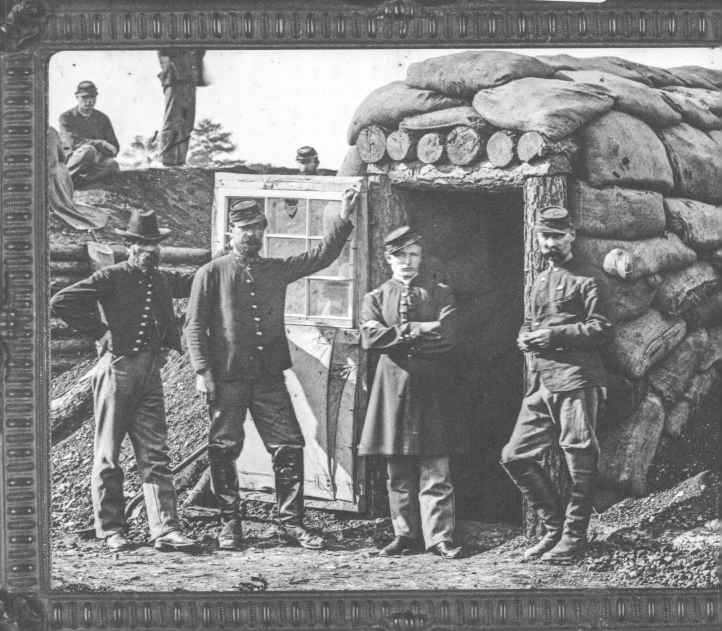

MARK SCEURMAN AND MARK MORAN
AUTHORS OF *WEIRD U.S.*, PRESENT

WEIRD
CIVIL
WAR

YOUR TRAVEL GUIDE TO THE GHOSTLY LEGENDS AND
BEST-KEPT SECRETS OF THE AMERICAN CIVIL WAR

STERLING
New York

STERLING
New York

An Imprint of Sterling Publishing
1166 Avenue of the Americas
New York, NY 10036

ISBN 978-1-4549-1579-9

Distributed in Canada by Sterling Publishing
c/o Canadian Manda Group, 664 Annette Street
Toronto, Ontario, Canada M6S 2C8
Distributed in the United Kingdom by GMC Distribution Services
Castle Place, 166 High Street, Lewes, East Sussex, England BN7 1XU
Distributed in Australia by Capricorn Link (Australia) Pty. Ltd.
P.O. Box 704, Windsor, NSW 2756, Australia

Book design and production:
gonzalez defino, ny / gonzalezdefino.com

For information about custom editions, special sales,
and premium and corporate purchases,
please contact Sterling Special Sales at 800-805-5489
or specialsales@sterlingpublishing.com.

Manufactured in China

6 8 10 9 7 5

Weird Civil War is intended as entertainment to present a historical record of local legends,
folklore, and sites related to the Civil War throughout the United States. Many of these
legends and stories cannot be independently confirmed or corroborated, and the authors
and publisher make no representation of their factual accuracy. The reader should be advised
that many of the sites described in *Weird Civil War* are located on private property
and such sites should not be visited, or you may be prosecuted for trespassing.

www.sterlingpublishing.com

TICE W FURROW
VIRGINIA
PVT CO 14 VIRGINIA RES
CIVIL WAR

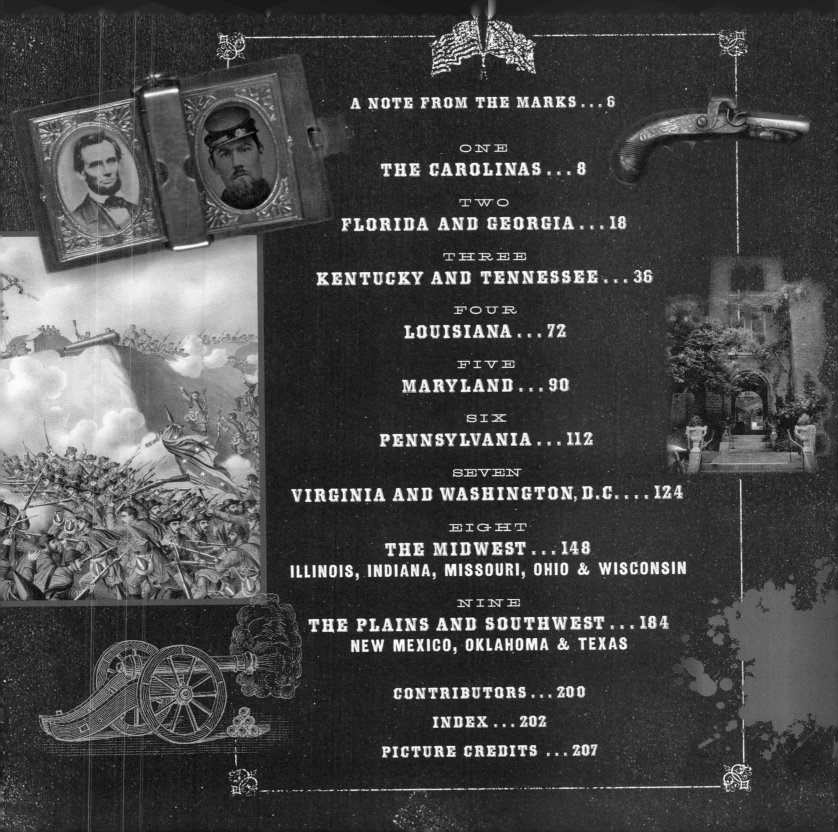

A NOTE FROM THE MARKS

Our weird journey began a long, long time ago in a far-off land called New Jersey. Once a year or so, we'd compile a homespun newsletter called *Weird N.J.*, then pass it on to our friends. The pamphlet was a collection of odd news clippings, bizarre facts, little-known historical anecdotes, and anomalous encounters from our home state. The newsletter also included the kinds of localized legends that were often whispered around a particular town but seldom heard outside the boundaries of the community where they originated.

We had started *Weird N.J.* on the simple theory that every town in the state had at least one good tale to tell. The publication soon became a full-fledged magazine, and we made the decision to actually do our own investigating to see if we could track down where all of these seemingly unbelievable stories were coming from. Was there, we wondered, any factual basis for the fantastic local legends people were telling us about? Armed with not much more than a camera and a notepad, we set off on a mystical journey of discovery. Much to our surprise and amazement, a lot of what we had initially presumed to be nothing more than urban legends turned out to be real—or at least to contain a grain of truth, which had sparked the lore to begin with.

After a dozen years of documenting the bizarre, we were asked to write a book about our adventures, and so *Weird N.J.: Your Travel Guide to New Jersey's Local Legends and Best Kept Secrets* was published in 2003. Soon people from all over the country began writing to us, telling us strange tales from their home state. As it turned out, what we had perceived to be something of very local interest was actually just a small part of a larger and more universal phenomenon. When our publisher asked us what we wanted to do next, the answer was simple: "We'd like to do a book called *Weird U.S.*, in which we could document the local legends and strangest stories from all over the country," we replied. So for the next twelve months, we set out in search of weirdness wherever it might be found in the fifty states. And indeed, we found plenty of it!

After *Weird U.S.* was published, we came to the conclusion that this country had more great tales than could be contained in just one book. Everywhere we looked, we found unwritten folklore, creepy cemeteries, cursed locations, and outlandish roadside oddities. With this in mind, we told our publisher that we wanted to document it all and to do it in a series of books, each focusing on the peculiarities of a particular state.

As the nation commemorates the sesquicentennial of the Civil War (1861–65), we assembled a collection of unexpected stories that arose from the War Between the States. Hundreds of thousands died on both sides during the conflict, and tales of ghosts and martial apparitions still resonate on battlefield sites and in cemeteries. And, to be sure, we've included a number of them in this volume. War is one of the most extreme circumstances that can be imagined by humanity, and as such is prone to incite some incredibly unusual situations and behavior in people. The stories you will find in the pages of this book are just some of the strange tales that were born of this horrendous conflict. Whether your sympathies are Union or Confederate, we hope you'll enjoy this journey back in time to a war that continues to bear a profound impact on the psyche of all of us as Americans.

Mark Sceurman, *left*, and Mark Moran, *right*, at the burial site of Stonewall Jackson's arm at Ellwood Manor, Fredricksburg & Spotsylvania National Military Park, VA.

We would like to thank all of the great Weird U.S. authors, photographers, and illustrators who contributed their talents to help bring this volume to life. We would also like to acknowledge the submissions of all of our wonderful readers from across this great country, on both sides of the Mason–Dixon Line, who have written letters suggesting stories to us and have shared their own personal tales of weirdness. *– Mark and Mark*

CHAPTER ONE

THE CAROLINAS

FLAGS OF FORT SUMTER

The attack on Fort Sumter in the mouth of Charleston Harbor, SC, at 4:30 sharp on the morning of April 12, 1861, is usually said to be the start of the Civil War. In reality, civil war was in the air many years before it started, as the states increasingly disagreed over a number of issues, especially slavery. The fort, held by Union forces under the command of Major Robert Anderson, held out for thirty-four hours of intense Confederate bombardment before finally surrendering.

At the time of the surrender, the flag that usually flew over the fort had been damaged, and a smaller version of Old Glory, called the Storm Flag, was flying. Anderson had been given permission by his victors to lower the flag with one last hundred-gun salute. During the salute, a spark set off an explosion that killed Union private Daniel Hough and seriously injured several other members of the gun crew. Hough was the only fatality of the Battle of Fort Sumter. Anderson called off the salute at fifty guns, the Storm Flag was lowered and folded, Hough was quickly buried, and the Union soldiers were taken off the island.

Soldiers from a militia unit called the Palmetto Guard immediately raised the first Southern flag to be flown over conquered territory. Not exactly "flown," perhaps, because the Storm Flag's pole had been taken down in order to lower it, so Private John S. Byrd Jr., of the Palmetto Guard, draped the flag over the upper ramparts of the fort. This flag featured a green palmetto tree and a red star against a white background. The tree had been a symbol of South Carolinian resilience ever since the Revolutionary battle of Fort Moultrie, when British cannonballs had bounced off or sunk harmlessly into the tough, fibrous palmetto logs that formed Moultrie's walls. It is still featured on the state flag today.

The Storm Flag, also known as the Fort Sumter Flag, is now on display at Fort Sumter National Monument's museum, facing the old Palmetto Guard flag that replaced it. Both flags are ragged remnants of their former

Previous pages: The First National Flag of the Confederacy, or Stars and Bars, flying over Fort Sumter, April 16, 1861.

Telegram from Major Robert Anderson to U.S. secretary of war Simon Cameron, announcing his withdrawal from Fort Sumter, April 18, 1861.

☛ "If you look just as carefully to the right of the trunk on the old Palmetto Guard flag, you can also make out another faint image, stained into the weave of what was once its snow-white field, now dingy with age. It is an almost photographic image of a face."

selves, torn to shreds by artillery, wind, and the passage of time. And each contains a mystery. Two soldiers who played a historic role at Fort Sumter seem to have somehow transposed their images into the two old flags.

If you look carefully just to the right of the centermost star on the Storm Flag, a small patch has somehow lost its original deep blue dye and now looks just like the silhouetted image of a Union soldier. Some say it's the image of Private Hough, and it appeared there the day he died in the salute. And if you look just as carefully to the right of the trunk on the old Palmetto Guard flag, you can also make out another faint image, stained into the weave of what was once its snow-white field, now dingy with age. It is an almost photographic image of a face—could it be Private Byrd? If so, that would certainly make for a nice symmetry. Perhaps the voices sometimes heard at the fort are those of their spirits still trying to sort it all out, one asking the other why it took exactly four years for Hough, who witnessed the surrender and then died that day, to win in the end, while Byrd, who triumphed, to ultimately lose. When the war began, most folks guessed that at most it would last only four months. But wars often have a way of getting out of hand.

✳ **Fort Sumter National Monument, 1214 Middle St., Sullivan's Island, SC 29482, (843) 883-3123, www.nps.gov/fosu/contacts.htm**

The Storm Flag, *top*; on the Palmetto Flag, *center* and *bottom*, the image some believe is Private Byrd is faint, but it becomes much more distinct as contrast is increased.

HEADLESS BODIES OF FOLLY BEACH

In an October 27, 2005, article in the *Journal of James Island and Folly Beach*, SC, Sally Watts described how fourteen bodies were found in May 1987 when foundations for a construction site at the west end of Folly Beach were excavated. Construction was halted for a month while authorities investigated the remains.

According to Watts, "All of the bodies except one had been buried with shoulders directed to the west. Twelve of the bodies were missing skulls and other major body parts. Some of the burials had coffins; others had only ponchos. With the bodies were found Union army eagle buttons, one '#5' insignia from a cap, and Enfield Rifle .57 caliber Mini Balls."

State archaeologists finally decided the men were from the Union army's all-black 55th Massachusetts Volunteer Infantry Regiment.

"Because the bodies had no injuries, the possibility of death in battle was eliminated. That left only the possibility of death by illness, head injury, or beheading.

"There are several (unproven) opinions as to why the remains were minus [their] skulls. One theory is that bounty hunters sought the skulls of buried Union soldiers when the federal government offered rewards for retrieval of bodies. But the odd thing was that while the skulls were missing, the rest of the bones were undisturbed. . . . It's not likely bounty hunters would be so respectful when 'collecting' their prizes. Another opinion was that the skulls were removed by local islanders for voodoo rituals."

A final, even scarier, and perhaps more likely theory imagined a scene in which a deranged Confederate commander took things into his own hands, dispensed with official military regulations regarding the proper treatment of his prisoners, and ordered their heads cut off.

✺ **Folly River Park, Center St., Folly Beach, SC 29439**

An illustration from *Harper's Weekly* of the 55th Massachusetts Volunteer Infantry Regiment marching in Charleston later in the war, February 21, 1865.

The ruins of the Chapel of Ease at St. Helena Parish, St. Helena Island, photographed in the mid-twentieth century.

LAND'S END LIGHT

Undoubtedly the most well-known mystery light in South Carolina is the one that appears along old Land's End Road on St. Helena Island, near Beaufort. This light has been seen since the Civil War. Legend has it that the light is a beheaded ghost with a lantern, said to be a Confederate soldier who was jumped by some Yankee ne'er-do-wells and suffered the loss of his thinker in the melee that erupted. Other stories say it was a Federal soldier ambushed by brave rebels who lopped off his head when he besmirched their family honor. Or else it was an escaped slave. Or a Spaniard. Or a lost lover. In the end, perhaps it doesn't matter—something is out there at night throwing a glow and causing a stir.

If you want to see the Land's End Light, go to the village of Frogmore on St. Helena Island and turn south on Land's End Road. Not too long after you pass the campus of the Penn Center, you'll come to the ghostly ruins of the 1740s' Chapel of Ease. After darkness falls, this is a good place to stop and look for strange lights. Orb watchers will find plenty of activity to keep them occupied, both in the ruins of the chapel and around a sadly vandalized mausoleum that looks like a miniature Egyptian temple.

If you don't have any luck here, head on past Adam Street Baptist Church and then pull off the road. You won't be able to see the old Hanging Tree from here if it's really dark—it's even farther down the road—but this is the most likely place to encounter the light. You have to be patient and quiet. In the summer, be sure to bring some mosquito repellant.

We should add a word of warning. If you do see the light looming down the road, just stay put and enjoy it. Don't make the same mistake as some folks who have attempted to drive toward it or through it. Several years ago, some off-duty marines from nearby Parris Island were killed when they tried this and slammed into a tree.

✳ **Chapel of Ease ruins, 17 Lands End Rd., St. Helena Island, SC 29920**

LOCAL LEGEND

When some people in Darlington, SC, talk about the Civil War, they don't talk about troop movements or battles. They like to single out the story of Union soldier J. L. Klickner. He was ordered by General Sherman to burn the home of Confederate Colonel Samuel H. Wilds. Klickner was unable to bring himself to do it. Why? It turns out that before the war he had been an architect, and the Wilds home had been one of his fondest commissions. He just couldn't bring himself to destroy his own labor of love. This nonevent has become a local legend in ways that reveal far more about the complexities of that conflict than any straight historical record could.

YANKEE IN A REBEL TOWN

There's a whopper of a mistake standing in the center of Kingstree, SC. According to Linda Brown, editor of the *News* there, the Confederate monument next to the Williamsburg County Courthouse really is a Yankee soldier.

"The story we've always heard is that somehow it got mixed up with the monument that was to go to York, Maine. So York has Johnny Reb and we have the Yankee soldier. . . . Many Civil War buffs have stopped by my office to ask if we were aware of the Yankee soldier at the courthouse.

✪ **Confederate Monument, Main St., Kingstree, SC 29556**

A Yankee stands on the Confederate Monument in Kingstree, SC.

HUNLEY CREWS

mong the some 2,300 Confederate soldiers buried at Magnolia Cemetery in Charleston are all three crews of the *H. L. Hunley*, considered the world's first "successful" submarine (though the men who drowned while hand cranking her propeller during her various voyages may have thought otherwise). The *Hunley* itself disappeared after its last run, during which it sank the Union warship *Housatonic*, and was rediscovered in 1995. The remains of the crew from that voyage were buried in Magnolia in 2004. The submarine is now undergoing a multimillion-dollar restoration.

✵ **Magnolia Cemetery, 70 Cunnington Ave., Charleston, SC 29405, (843) 722-8638, www.magnoliacemetery.net; open daily 8 a.m.–5 p.m.**

A recent photograph of the graves of *Hunley* crewmen at Magnolia Cemetery in Charleston.

WEEPING ARCH OF NEW BERN

Visitors beware of walking under the Weeping Arch at the entrance to the Cedar Grove Cemetery in New Bern.

Cedar Grove Cemetery is easily the most haunted place in the smallish coastal city of New Bern, NC. Graves dating back to the early 1800s fill the huge, undulating space, in the center of which is an unusual mass grave containing the remains of at least three hundred Confederate soldiers who died during the battle to save the city. What makes it unusual, at least for the South, is that it's an ossuary—the soldiers were originally buried directly in the battlefield, wherever they'd fallen, but years later their bones were retrieved and transferred to Cedar Grove.

Citizens of New Bern know better than to linger for long under the peculiar triple arch leading into their cemetery. The Weeping Arch, as they call it, is made of marl, a porous conglomerate of compacted fossil seashells, which absorbs moisture from rain and everyday humidity and drips almost constantly. If one of the drops ever falls on you, they believe, you'll be returning to visit Cedar Grove again quite soon, and . . . dead!

✳ **Cedar Grove Cemetery, between Howard and George Sts., New Bern, NC 28562**

GHOSTLY HANDS BELOW THE BRIDGE

The Greene Street Bridge in Greenville, NC, has had a problem ever since local men first spotted hands emerging from the waters below it many years ago. Depending on who you talk to, they belong to a fisherman who drowned here years ago or to someone who committed suicide by jumping off the bridge. If you climb down along the riverbank and go up under the roadway and listen carefully, you can still hear dying gasps and screams echoing from the underside of the bridge.

However, if you do this, stay well away from the water's edge. Several years ago, some kids heard the screams and stepped a little too close to the Tar River to investigate, when a pair of "nasty, shriveled-up-looking hands" came up out of the water and grabbed one boy's ankles and snatched him under. His pals ran to get help, but the body was never recovered.

Several scuba divers have told Roger Kammerer that there is a headless statue of a Civil War soldier jammed into the mud beneath the bridge, but they haven't figured out how to free it and bring it to the surface safely. Whether it has anything to do with the pair of grasping hands that reach up out of the water from time to time nobody seems to know. Maybe he's really looking for a replacement head and keeps trying on for size anything he can reach.

✳ **Due to structural issues, the bridge was moved and converted to a pedestrian bridge in the town commons.**

"Don't Mock This Road!"

A soldier once stationed in the South, who uses the e-mail moniker CoutuJA, describes an encounter with what may have been the ghost of a Civil War soldier.

"Highway 24 runs through Jacksonville, NC, and past Camp Lejeune, and this stretch is said to have been a Civil War trail used by the Union army. It is also where the Union army slaughtered a whole company of Confederate soldiers. Many locals believe it is haunted.

"While stationed at Camp Lejeune, I witnessed plenty of weirdness in my many late-night travels on this road. One time I was right in front of the base's front gates when my car's headlights dimmed and the sounds on the radio faded to nothing. At first I thought my car was breaking down, but then something much stranger happened: The gas pedal hit the floor all by itself and the

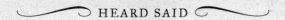

☞ "Over the radio
I heard a faint voice saying,
'Damn the living
who mock this road!'"

car took off toward a tree. It was about to slam into the tree when it suddenly came to a dead stop. And over the radio I heard a faint voice saying, 'Damn the living who mock this road!'

"Was I hearing the voice of a long-dead Confederate soldier? I'll never know, but I'll also never forget what happened that night." ~*CoutuJA*

✳ **Marine Corps Base Camp Lejeune,
33 Holcomb Blvd., Alabama Ave.,
Camp Lejeune, NC 28547, (910) 451-1113,
www.lejeune.marines.mil**

The front gate at
Camp Lejeune, where
strange goings-on
have occurred.

 CHAPTER TWO

FLORIDA AND GEORGIA

SEARCHING FOR LEWIS POWELL'S HEAD {AND THE REST OF HIM}

In the Geneva community cemetery in Seminole County, FL, beneath the shade of a half-dozen old cypress trees, is a rather peculiar grave containing only a skull. It's all that remains of Lewis Thornton Powell. Whether he was a villain or a hero largely depends on which side of the Mason-Dixon Line you're on. Lewis Powell, you see, was a Florida Confederate soldier and a conspirator in the assassination of Abraham Lincoln. So, you may wonder, why is only his head buried in a little cemetery northeast of Orlando?

Lewis Powell was the youngest son of Reverend George and Patience Caroline Powell's eight children. The family had lived in Alabama and Georgia before settling in Live Oak, FL. At the outbreak of the Civil War, the seventeen-year-old Lewis enlisted in the 2nd Florida Infantry in Jasper. Two of his brothers, George and Oliver, also served in the Confederate army. George survived the war, but Oliver returned home crippled.

Lewis suffered a wound to his wrist at Gettysburg, where he was captured by Union troops and sent to a prison hospital in Baltimore. In September 1863, only two weeks after arriving at the hospital, he escaped and made his way to Virginia, where he joined Mosby's Rangers of the 43rd Virginia Cavalry Battalion. The records indicate that Lewis Powell's service with the Virginia cavalry was "distinctive." However, in January 1865, he deserted from this unit and crossed to the Union side. Using an alias, Lewis Paine, he took the Oath of Allegiance to the Union.

There is strong speculation among historians that Powell switched sides and changed his name because 🖛

Previous pages: The 4th Georgia Volunteer Infantry, Company K, April 1861.

Lewis Powell in wrist irons on the USS *Saugus*, where several of the Lincoln assassination conspirators were incarcerated, photographed by Alexander Gardner, April 1865.

The execution of Mary Surratt, Lewis
Powell, David Herold, and George Atzerodt,
photographed by Alexander Gardner, July 7, 1865.

"No one knows what became of the rest of him or how his head ended up with Indian bones at the Smithsonian. Perhaps the rest of his skeleton is still stored in a dark corner of some Washington warehouse."

he was a secret Confederate agent. It is known that he became involved with John Wilkes Booth in a scheme to kidnap Abraham Lincoln. The plan was to trade Lincoln for Confederate prisoners of war, but when the mission did not work as planned, Booth hatched his infamous plot to assassinate the president and other high-level Union officials. Lewis Powell was recruited for this mission, along with David Herold, George Atzerodt, and Mary Surratt.

Each conspirator had a specific role in the mission. Booth was to shoot the president at the same time that Powell was to kill Secretary of State William Seward. In order for Powell to do his part, he had to go to the home of Seward, who was recuperating in bed from a carriage accident.

On the evening of April 14, 1865, Booth shot Lincoln at Ford's Theatre. But Powell and Herold ran into unexpected difficulty at the Seward home. Four people were stabbed inside the house before Powell could make his way up to Seward's bedroom. He stabbed the bedridden secretary of state several times and then in a panic ran from the house. Seward survived the attack but was left disfigured for life.

After evading authorities for three days, Powell showed up disguised as a laborer at the home of co-conspirator Mary Surratt. Unfortunately for him, he arrived at the very time Surratt was being arrested, and he was taken into custody as well.

At his trial, Lewis Powell sat like a statue while his attorney, W. E. Doster, argued his innocence by claiming, "He lives in that land of imagination where it seems to him legions of southern soldiers wait to crown him as their chief commander." Instead of a coronation, though, Lewis and his fellow conspirators were hanged on July 7, 1865, in the courtyard of the Old Arsenal Building in Washington. In 1869, all the bodies were claimed by relatives for reburial except the body of Lewis Powell, which remained in a lone grave.

Meanwhile, back in Florida, the Powell family, fearing retaliation after a Jacksonville newspaper exposed them as relatives of a Lincoln assassination conspirator, moved from Live Oak to the rural seclusion of what is now Oviedo, then in Orange County.

Lewis Powell's body was reburied at least once in the Washington area, but later his remains mysteriously became lost. In 1992, his skull, identified by museum catalogue numbers, was discovered among American Indian skeletal remains in the Smithsonian's Museum of Natural History. No one knows what became of the rest of him or how his head ended up with Indian bones at the Smithsonian. Perhaps the rest of his skeleton is still stored in a dark corner of some Washington warehouse.

The Smithsonian located his closest living relative, Helen Alderman of Geneva, FL, and released the skull to her. Using her own funds, she arranged a proper interment. On November 12, 1994, in a Confederate memorial service, a small mahogany box containing Lewis Thornton Powell's skull was buried next to his mother's grave in the Old Geneva Cemetery.

Geneva Cemetery, Cemetery Rd., Geneva, FL 32732

THE MAN WHO LOST THE WAR?

One of the Civil War's greatest generals is also one of its most controversial. Georgian James "Pete" Longstreet was beloved by Robert E. Lee, who called him "My Old Warhorse." Longstreet fought throughout the war from Manassas to Appomattox and was instrumental in most Confederate victories. However, some believe that he cost the South ultimate success in the crucial battle at Gettysburg. An honest study of the battle reveals the shortcomings of many Confederate leaders, including the sainted Lee, who was man enough to accept full responsibility for the fatal defeat and offered his resignation. However, after Lee's death, a conspiracy of Virginia generals sought to sanctify Lee and chose Longstreet, a non-Virginian, as a scapegoat. According to this theory, Longstreet unaccountably delayed his attack on July 2, costing Lee a victory and, ultimately, the war itself.

Longstreet retired to Gainesville, where he owned a hotel and vineyard. At his death in 1904, surviving Confederate officials refused to attend his funeral, but his soldiers, who knew the truth, attended en masse. Longstreet is buried in Gainesville's Alta Vista Cemetery, where visitors pay homage by contributing to the general's favorite vices, leaving cigars and whiskey bottles (usually empty) at his grave.

Alta Vista Cemetery, 521 Jones St., Gainesville, GA 30503, (770) 535-6883, www.gainesville.org/alta-vista-cemetery

"Longstreet was beloved by Robert E. Lee, who called him 'My Old Warhorse.'"

General James Longstreet, ca. 1862.

OLUSTEE'S REENACTING REVENANT ☞ *Charlie Carlson*

Florida's largest Civil War battle was fought on February 20, 1864, at Olustee. It was at this bloody spot in North Florida that General Joseph Finegan's 5,200 Confederates blocked Union general Truman Seymour's advancing army. Seymour planned to march his 5,000 mostly black troops westbound across the state to cut transportation lines from central Florida that were funneling supplies to the Confederate forces in northern Georgia.

General Seymour had been warned by a defiant Southern woman, "Y'all will come back faster than you go." He found the woman's rant amusing, unaware it was a premonition of the fate awaiting his Federal forces. The Battle of Olustee ended with a Confederate victory that left the woods scattered with the corpses of 203 Yankees and 93 rebels.

Many of the battlefield dead were hastily buried in a makeshift cemetery. Stories about wild hogs rooting up the graves and eating the bodies persist. Other folk tales casually mention people picking up scattered bones as souvenirs of the battle. Unsubstantiated or not, such stories are bound to rouse a few spirits.

In 1912, a historical monument was erected at the battle site, and for the past few decades a large reenactment has been held each February to commemorate the battle. Thousands of spectators flock to Olustee to watch reenactors bring the past alive, and it seems at times they have some paranormal help.

👉 "It really got me wondering. . . . Maybe that guy had never seen cellophane; maybe he was in another time zone and somehow our paths got crossed up, because whatever happened to his campfire is beyond me."

Orbs and ectoplasma ribbons of light have been caught in both digital and 35mm photos taken over the battlefield and during the event's annual Civil War Ball. Darting and floating orbs have appeared twice in video footage. To those who feel orbs are dust particles kicked up during reenactments, there's evidence that cannot be tied to dust, such as electronic voice phenomenon (EVP) recordings made at the site and fleeting glimpses of translucent apparitions in the pine forest surrounding the historic battlefield.

AN AUTHENTIC ENCOUNTER

While playing dead during the mock battle, one reenactor recalled having an "eerie feeling" and "hearing a discarnate voice" that kept repeating, "Have you seen the elephant?"—a Civil War euphemism for experiencing combat. Another instance involves Ray Barlow, who in 2002 was helping a friend who worked as a sutler (vendor) at Civil War events set up before the Olustee reenactment. When they finished, Ray decided to walk along a trail that, he said, led to a very authentic encounter:

I get a good ways down the trail and see this guy decked out in Confederate garb. I mean, he really looked the part, and on top of that he was barefooted. He was sitting next to a pine tree and had a small campfire going. So, he says, "Howdy," and I answered back but noticed he looked pretty skinny, like really ragged. I mean, he really looked the part. Of course, the reenactment wasn't until the next day.

Anyway, he asked if I had a "chaw," so I pulled a square of chewing tobacco out of my shirt pocket. A lot of reenactors chew and spit—it adds realism to the whole business of reenacting. I handed it to him and he unwrapped the cellophane, cut off a plug with his knife, and put it in his mouth. Then he held the cellophane up and looked through it at the sun. He studied it for a bit and then asked me, "What's this made of?"

I said, "It's cellophane." I figured he was making fun of me, having something that didn't fit the period theme. He didn't say much, but asked if he could have a piece of that cellophane. I obliged his request, put the tobacco back in my pocket, and went on down the trail.

Thirty minutes later, Ray went back to the spot by the tree to find no trace of the man—or the campfire. He told a friend about his experience, joking that he'd seen a ghost. Ray didn't see the man for the rest of the weekend, and when he got home, he looked up information on cellophane and learned it hadn't been invented until 1908.

"It really got me wondering," Ray said. "Maybe that guy had never seen cellophane; maybe he was in another time zone and somehow our paths got crossed up, because whatever happened to his campfire is beyond me."

✹ **Olustee Battlefield State Park, U.S. 90, Olustee, FL 32072, (386) 758-0400, www.floridastateparks.org/Olustee**

A recent image of reenactors at the Olustee Battlefield Historic State Park; the battle is reenacted annually every February.

THE WAR'S ONLY WAR CRIMINAL

Andersonville Prison in Sumter County ranks as one of America's greatest tragedies. Designed for 10,000 Union soldiers, it was occupied by more than 45,000, and 13,000 died of disease, malnutrition, and polluted water. For a while, the camp was terrorized by a group of prisoners called the Raiders, who stole food and killed any who dared oppose them. Those despicable men were arrested and tried by their fellow inmates. Six were executed, their graves separated from honorable soldiers.

The original commandant of Andersonville died before war's end, so his replacement, Henry Wirz, was held to account. A kangaroo court held in Washington, D.C., convicted Wirz of various crimes, and he was executed and buried in Mount Olivet Cemetery.

Opposite: The still-controversial Wirz Monument in downtown Andersonville; it was dedicated by the United Daughters of the Confederacy on May 12, 1909.

Andersonville Prison as it stood on August 17, 1864.

The tiny village of Andersonville sits not even a mile away from the Andersonville National Cemetery and prison site. Believing Wirz innocent of any crime, a substantial monument was raised there for his vindication by the United Daughters of the Confederacy. The Civil War's only war criminal is honored near the site of the horrors of Andersonville.

In the cemetery is the grave of the first prisoner to die at Andersonville, Adam Swarner, in grave 1. (His brother was buried in grave 4,005.) The only decorated stone, bearing a peace dove, belongs to L. S. Tuttle (12,196). Other Federals who died in Georgia were reburied here following the war, including John Rupert (13,696) and John Hines (13,697)—the last soldiers killed in the war. They were victims of friendly fire during the capture of Jefferson Davis at Irwinville.

Andersonville National Historic Site, 760 POW Rd., Andersonville, GA 31711, www.nps.gov/ande; open daily 8 a.m.–5 p.m.

JINGLE BELLS YANKEE OR REBEL?

James Pierpont was born in Medford, Massachusetts, where his father was pastor of Hollis Street Church. James went to sea at fourteen and later headed for California to seek his fortune. He returned home penniless and in poor health. Next he traveled to Savannah, where his brother was pastor at Savannah Unitarian Church, to conduct music and give lessons. It was there that he began writing songs in the style of Stephen Foster.

Despite the fact that his father was an ardent abolitionist, James joined the 1st Georgia Cavalry and wrote the stirring Confederate songs "We Conquer or Die!" and "Strike for the South." But his most famous tune, one recognized worldwide, was titled "One Horse Open Sleigh." We know it as "Jingle Bells."

A minor civil war has raged in recent decades as Medford and Savannah both claim the song. While Pierpont copyrighted the song in Savannah in 1857, there is evidence that it may be considerably older. In Medford, he had made the acquaintance of a boarder at Mrs. Otis Waterman's boardinghouse—one William Webber, who operated a music school. He allowed Pierpont to use his piano for practice and composing songs. After a particularly delightful sleigh race between Medford and a neighboring town in 1850, Pierpont was inspired, says Thalia Shurtleff, a Massachusetts researcher. "This composer sat down at the piano and pecked out a tune on it. The song was an immediate hit in Medford and was often sung on sleigh rides that winter."

Hold your horses, Savannah responds. It maintains that one Christmas, James was searching for a happy song for youngsters in the church. Perhaps in a fit of

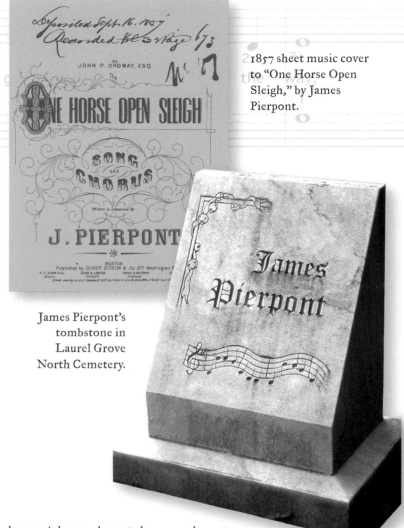

1857 sheet music cover to "One Horse Open Sleigh," by James Pierpont.

James Pierpont's tombstone in Laurel Grove North Cemetery.

homesickness, he sat down and wrote the tune. In 1985, a historical marker was erected in Troup Square near the church, and Savannah officially declared "Jingle Bells" a local tune.

Which story is true? No one is really sure. But Savannah has the last word—or note. James Pierpont rests in that city's Laurel Grove North Cemetery, where his monument is engraved with the opening notes of "Jingle Bells."

✺ **Laurel Grove North Cemetery, 802 W. Anderson St., Savannah, GA 31415; open daily 8 a.m.–5 p.m.**

SPIRIT IDENTIFIES FALLEN SOLDIERS

After the Civil War, many communities "adopted" the graves of unknown soldiers, lavishing them with care and ceremony. Four graves in north Georgia were tended by employees of the Western and Atlantic Railroad.

Two of the graves, along the tracks near Adairsville, intrigued Alice B. Howell. During a table-tapping séance around 1939, Alice asked the spirits to identify the two Confederates. The table obliged and tapped out the names Jack Kirby and Tice Furrow. The spirit world, it turned out, knew its soldiers. Research in the National Archives confirmed the identity of Furrow, and the federal government supplied a regulation veterans' headstone. There were too many J. Kirbys for a definite identification, so Alice ordered a stone for that grave. On May 1, 1974, the comrades were reinterred at Adairsville's Eastview Cemetery in a ceremony attended by local, state, and federal officials.

Two Confederate graves remain at Allatoona Pass (in present-day Cartersville)—one to the south, the other to the north—and the railroad still cares for them. The most accessible is to the south, and the graves have generated several paranormal stories, including the wandering spirits of the men and a ghost dog that chases passing trains.

CONFEDERATE GRAVITY

In the city of Dalton, GA, there is a gravity hill located in the West Hill Cemetery. According to legend, if you put your car in neutral and turn off the headlights, your vehicle is mysteriously pushed up the incline. We don't know if this is relevant to the phenomenon, but the cemetery has a large Confederate section. Maybe squads of Men in Gray are providing the locomotion.

CAUTION: Putting your car in neutral at the bottom of a hill invites auto accidents. We don't recommend that any readers tempt fate by testing the irrefutable laws of physics. It's not only potentially hazardous; it's also illegal, so gravity wouldn't be the only law you'd be putting to the test.

The gravestones of Jack Kirby and Tice Furrow at the Eastview Cemetery in Adairsville.

GEORGIA'S CURSED PROPERTY

British-born Godfrey Barnsley immigrated to Savannah in the nineteenth century and made his fortune in the cotton trade, eventually owning a fleet of ships that traded goods between the United States and Europe. Because Savannah's climate promoted deadly diseases during half the year, Barnsley searched for a perfect location in the cool mountains for his beloved wife, Julia, and their children. He found his Eden in Bartow County, between Kingston and Adairsville, and purchased a vast estate of 3,600 acres in 1840.

Barnsley set out to construct a fine brick mansion, which he named Woodlands. The home, designed in the Italianate style, rose to three stories and contained twenty-eight rooms. He ordered a stove that could provide food for 150 guests and a huge mahogany dining table from Brazil, capable of sitting forty. On their journeys around the world, Barnsley's ships gathered Italian marble, English doors and paneling, and unique plants and trees from several continents.

The property surrounding Woodlands was as elegant as the house, featuring acres of luxuriant English boxwoods, five thousand aquatic plants in a bog garden, one hundred varieties of roses, an Oriental garden, rock gardens, goldfish ponds, and exquisite statues.

The grand estate took decades to construct, but sadly, Julia died in 1845, three years before its completion. Although devastated, Godfrey continued the project. He frequently visited the boxwood gardens, lingering near a twelve-foot-high fountain, where he communed with the spirit of his wife, who directed work from beyond the grave.

Ten years after Julia's death, Godfrey received a letter from his father-in-law, who had also passed on a decade earlier. "My dear mortal Barnsley," it began, "Julia is with me and all doing just fine." It was signed William Scarborough II and was in the deceased's handwriting. 🖛

Left and *opposite*: The ruins of the Woodlands Mansion.

"*My dear mortal Barnsley . . .*"

> ☛ "There was definitely something here when we got here—there was something. I had a funny feeling inside—I can't explain it. It was kind of a nervousness, like butterflies in my stomach, like a cold sweat."

But all was not fine in this realm. The Barnsley family and Woodlands seemed cursed. Four of Godfrey's children died prematurely. When the Civil War erupted, Barnsley invested his fortune in Confederate bonds and lost everything except his beloved Woodlands.

Over the next several decades, family members struggled to keep the place up, but they and subsequent heirs were required to sell much of the property to settle debts. In 1906, a tornado tore the roof off the mansion, forcing the family to live in the detached kitchen. Tragically, in 1935 a Barnsley great-grandson murdered his brother there.

When Godfrey Barnsley purchased his property, departing Native Americans had warned him that the land had been cursed by its former Cherokee owner. It was a warning the confident merchant had ignored, and many believe it was the origin of his misfortunes.

For half a century, Woodlands was abandoned, the mansion disappearing beneath trees and brush. In the 1980s, European investors purchased 1,600 acres, cleared the historic area, and constructed a golf community. Visitors are welcome to wander through the reconstructed gardens and gaze at the magnificent ruins of Woodlands. A museum in the detached kitchen explores the history of the Barnsley family and their land. On the floor are preserved bloodstains from the murdered brother.

The new owners brought in Cherokee Indians from Oklahoma and North Carolina to bless the property. "There was definitely something here when we got here—there was something," Richard Bird, a Cherokee medicine man told reporters. "I had a funny feeling inside—I can't explain it. It was kind of a nervousness, like butterflies in my stomach, like a cold sweat." He personally believed that cast magic dies with its originator, but he proceeded "just to be on the safe side."

The curse seems to have been lifted. However, benign spirits remain. Julia's ghost is still sighted in the garden, particularly around the fountain, sometimes in the company of Godfrey. Three other Barnsley family members are also known to haunt the building and grounds, and a Confederate colonel, in full uniform, is occasionally glimpsed.

✳ **Barnsley Gardens, 597 Barnsley Gardens Rd., Adairsville, GA 30103, (770) 773-7480, www.barnsleyresort.com**

A COMPLEX HAUNTING ☞ *Joanne M. Austin*

John and Holly Quinn moved to McDonough, GA, in 1999, thinking the quiet city would offer a nice change of pace after living in Atlanta. When the couple bought a mobile home in a complex not far from Route 75, they didn't realize it was located in the heart of Ghost Central. According to John, just two weeks after moving in the couple started hearing "footsteps in the home, and disembodied voices," and seeing "all kinds of unusual lights out in the yard and in the home."

Supernatural encounters involving Civil War soldiers are common fare at the Quinns' home. Although John hasn't really "seen" the soldiers, except in some photographs a psychic took, Holly, who is clairvoyant, has. She was in the kitchen one day before heading off to work when she sensed someone coming into the room from the hallway. She thought it was John, but as she turned around, John says, she saw "a full-fledged soldier in the hallway here, in full uniform." Even more, she felt "he wanted to be seen by her." Another soldier told Holly his name was Silas Adams and that he was one of the entities responsible for the unusual events occurring in her home.

Many people doubt these "soldier" ghost stories. The county historian told John that there were no battles where the complex is situated today, and thus no scenes of mass carnage that might have spawned a few ghosts. John, however, remains steadfast: "There were skirmishes through here. There had to be. Troop movement and everything."

Psychics have confirmed that two Civil War ghosts "are staying in the home." They've told the Quinns that it's a gateway entry where they've seen "hundreds and hundreds of troops, north and south, coming through" during General William T. Sherman's massive Atlanta Campaign.

PARANORMAL ENERGY

Like any good reporter looking for a seasonal ghost angle for the news, Josh Clark, editor of Georgia's *Henry County Times*, visited the Quinns' home in October 2004. In the story that ran later that month, Josh described his initial impression of the house: "When one enters their home . . . there is a dismal quality to be felt. It lies not in the decor of the house, nor any state of disarray, rather it seems to emanate from the home itself, or perhaps the ground on which the home is situated." ☛

Neighbors have also seen odd things. John recalls that one Sunday morning, when he was heading out to the store, a neighbor yelled to him: "Turn around quick! Look!" John did, and saw a little girl in a Victorian-era dress behind him. The little girl disappeared as fast as she had appeared. Another time, a neighbor wanted to take a picture of the street because a ghost had just been seen there. John left his car running to go help his neighbor. The next thing he knew, "My car's going in reverse and getting ready to hit a house. And I had to go running after it. . . ."

It's often thought that ghosts can't cause physical harm to the living. John feels differently, and with good cause. On one occasion, John was thrown headfirst into a trash can in their backyard. "Something had physically picked me up," he says, and put him in the trash. "I had sores on my side for a couple of weeks after that incident. My sister-in-law loves that story, though!"

John says there is still paranormal activity, even though his minister and a local priest have blessed the home several times. Burning sage helps keep the spirits at bay, at least temporarily: "When I start hearing the

An engraving from the January 7, 1865 edition of *Harper's Weekly* depicts Sherman's troops moving out of captured Atlanta on the March to the Sea that began on November 15, 1864—a period when "hundreds and hundreds of troops, north and south, [were] coming through" the region near the Quinns' home.

tapping and rapping going on, I get the sage stick out and I'll say, 'I'm going to fix you.' And as soon as I bless the home and say the 'Our Father' throughout the home, the tapping and all stops. It'll calm it down for maybe a month and it'll start all back over." John also recently learned that a friend's mother, who lives in the same complex, has had otherworldly encounters in her home. He hopes to get permission to investigate the scene and gather additional information on the resident hauntings.

What's causing the eerie events at the Quinns' home? Could it be the nearby train wreck from the 1900s, the unmarked graves on the property, or the Indian burial ground? Or maybe the previously mentioned Civil War campaign is the source of the spirit brigade. And if that's not enough, within eighteen feet of the Quinns' home is a power transformer—often thought to be a conduit for paranormal energy—and a network of underground streams have been detected, and they too have otherworldly associations. Still, others believe that the city of McDonough is in a vortex—or at least a site—of negative energy and that the hauntings are just by happenstance.

CHAPTER THREE

KENTUCKY
AND
TENNESSEE

BROTHERS IN ARMS SHARE A SPOOKY RIDE ☞ *Lee Jorgensen*

One night in 1994, as I made my way back from a bar in Louisville to the Army base at which I was stationed, I took a spectral hitchhiker for a short ride.

I didn't even know he was a ghost at first. I saw him on the side of the road in my headlights, stopped a little ways past him, reversed my car to where he stood and offered him a ride to the base, which was a good four or five miles off the highway. As he got into the car, I saw that he was wearing what I thought was an old Civil War outfit, complete with a sword. Since people in the area love the Civil War, I assumed he was part of a re-creation event and his outfit didn't bother me. I didn't even think it was odd that this was happening at three or four in the morning.

We drove not more than a mile or so. About one hundred feet after we crossed an overpass, the soldier picked up his sword and asked me to stop. I asked him if he was sure, and told him it was too cold to be walking the rest of the way to the base, which is where I assumed he wanted to go. Plus, I explained, if he was regular army he would have to be getting up in a few hours like the rest of us, and it was better if he just let me take him where he needed to go on base. He said no thanks, and that he appreciated the ride. He told me to have a safe trip.

So dressed in Confederate garb with hat, sword, and all, and very polite besides, he got out of my car. I looked in the passenger side mirror to see where he went and saw nothing. I looked on the other side of the car and saw more of the same. I put the car in reverse to use the backup lights and still saw nothing. I turned the car around and tried to use my headlights to see what I could see . . . nothing. There was nowhere else for the soldier to go and short grass for acres around the road, but he was gone.

I went home to my barracks and didn't think anything about it till the next day when I told my friends about what happened. They said I must have been drunk, but I'd only had a few drinks earlier that night and knew that I wasn't. And even though the drive from Louisville to the base took over an hour, I wasn't tired. I never ever thought that seeing a ghost would be something I might experience, but that's what happened to me that night on a Kentucky road.

Previous pages: Soldiers and civilians pose in front of the Citico Mound, a Mississippian burial mound in Chattanooga, TN, that became the site of a convalescent garden for wounded Union soldiers, 1864.

An unidentified Confederate soldier holding a sword, ca. 1862.

A recent photograph of the Talbott Tavern.

DOES JESSE JAMES HAUNT THE TALBOTT TAVERN?

Here's a real slice of Americana, and a severely spook-ridden one to boot. The Talbott Tavern in Bardstown, KY, built in 1779, is the oldest stagecoach-stop tavern and hotel in the United States. This building was well known as a must-visit place for anyone who happened to be passing through the area. Because of its central location at the junction of major stagecoach dirt roads, it was visited by practically everyone who traveled cross-country or to the frontier.

The main tavern area is preserved, looking mostly as it did then, with only a few modifications and modernizations. Everyone from presidents to kings to outlaws made camp here: Abraham Lincoln, Andrew Jackson, Henry Clay, William Henry Harrison, King Louis-Phillippe of France, Jesse James, Daniel Boone, and many more.

Although Jesse James's ghost is claimed by some to walk these halls, we see no reason to believe that he should haunt a tavern just because he used to drink here. Ghostly activity predates his death, and in fact, James himself may have had a paranormal experience at the tavern. One night he claimed that he saw the murals painted on the walls of an upstairs room coming to life, and in his panic he shot the walls full of holes. Then again, he may just have been hallucinating on a bad batch of bourbon.

Ghosts of children have been prevalent here over the years, as well as ghosts of mysterious old men in antiquated clothing and of a woman said to be a suicide victim. She hung herself with a rope suspended from the main tavern's chandelier. Although that chandelier, which once held candles, has since been retrofitted with electricity, it is still in use today.

The eerie upstairs hallways have had so many ghost sightings that the staff have become accustomed to them. Manager Jonathan Mattingly noted one guest who complained about the children laughing and running in and out of the room next door. "I had to break it to him that there were no other guests in the hotel that night," says Mattingly, "and certainly no children in the building." A small display in the upstairs foyer alerts guests to the potential for such hauntings, so caveat emptor: Don't ring the front desk if you hear the pitter-patter of little (dead) feet! ☛

A fire broke out upstairs at the Talbott Tavern in 1998 and destroyed the old wall murals that Jesse James had shot with lead. Though the paintings were ruined, the bullet holes are still there in the wall for all to see. It has been speculated that the cause of the fire could have been supernatural. Renovations are still ongoing, but whoever is working there will usually be glad to take you up to what is now called the Jesse James Room for a peek at the outlaw's handiwork.

Aside from the woman who took her own life, who's responsible for all these spirits shuffling around the tavern? Although it's almost a certainty that people died of illnesses and were murdered on the premises in the violent and chaotic frontier days of the eighteenth century, the most likely answer lies within two nearby buildings:

THE MCLEAN HOUSE
This handsome, circa 1812 brick building was once a post office and also a hospital that no doubt saw a lot of suffering, pain, and death, especially during the Civil War. Today it's a bed-and-breakfast.

THE JAILER'S INN
The city jail was conveniently located right next door to the tavern, and nowadays you can sleep here too. The structures of the jail cells have been left in their rustic and grim state, but fixed up somewhat and made into a very unusual inn. Original jailhouse graffiti still exists in some spots (including an elaborately painted winning poker hand). There's definitely a frightening and oppressive air to the building. You can't forget that you're in a jailhouse where many troubled souls lived and died over the span of two centuries. The Jailer's Inn is owned and operated by a local attorney who's happy to give tours to the curious. Like the Talbott Tavern, the inn is increasingly popular for "ghost tourism."

✴ **Talbott Tavern, 107 W. Stephen Foster Ave., Bardstown, KY 40004, (502) 348-3494, www.talbotts.com**

Opposite: Jesse James in 1864, the year he joined William Quantrille's Confederate guerrilla organization, which conducted raids along the Missouri-Kansas border.

A NOISY NIGHT AT THE TALBOTT INN

Recently my friend and I took a trip to Bardstown, and stayed for one night (and thankfully only one night) at a beautiful but haunted old stagecoach inn from 1779 called the Talbott Tavern & Inn. I had absolutely no idea the inn was haunted when I booked my stay there. (If I knew it was, I wouldn't have made the reservation; a ghost tour is one thing, spending the night with them is another.) I merely liked the idea that I could stay in a historical place where Jesse James hung out.

Well, the evening before we were scheduled to stay there we decided to have a drink at the tavern inside the inn. I started talking to the bartender, who after some discussion, told me that my friend and I were the only two people staying in the inn that following night, and that, "the ghosts will have someone to keep them company." I just shrugged off his comment as an attempt to scare us (my friend and I are both women). We checked into the Talbott in the General's Quarters at about 6 p.m., and I immediately felt as though someone was watching me, especially when I was taking a shower. After the innkeeper left (at about 7 p.m.), my friend went to grab our luggage as I got ready. I heard all kinds of banging noises outside the door to my room, but when I went to investigate (I used to be in law enforcement), there was no one there. My friend was still outside by the car. . . . I went back into the room and out of the corner of my eye I thought I saw a shadow move into the bathroom. I sat down in a chair in the room, but felt as though there was someone there with me. It's difficult to explain, but suffice to say it was uncomfortable enough that I had to get up and move.

After my friend brought the baggage up to the room, I saw yet something else strange, like a light coming from an upper corner of the room, across from the bathroom. At this point I decided to take out my contacts, and we went out to dinner—me with my hair still soaking wet, and without any makeup. I just didn't want to have to go back into the bathroom.

As it turned out, my friend ran into the innkeeper as she was outside gathering our luggage, and asked her if she could see some of the other rooms in the place, since she's a history buff too. The innkeeper just handed her a bunch of keys, and said that after she's done to leave them on the front desk—that they'll collect them in the morning. When we came home from dinner, the inn seemed to take on a more ominous feel. There were a lot of noises—banging, doors slamming shut, water turning on and off in unused rooms, the toilets flushing on their own, etc. So we decided to check out the other rooms in the "newer" (I think about 1815 or thereabouts) section of the inn. I found one room that had a very calm feeling to it, and was toasty warm (our room was warm, but very cold in spots, as was the Lincoln Room next door to the General's Quarters).

The minute we turned off the lights in our room, I heard the sound of a door slam shut loudly, a man sneeze, and then loud footsteps going down the hall. Then the door to our room banged a few times, as if someone grabbed the doorknob and tried to push the door open. Then I heard all kinds of noises throughout the rest of the inn— from a bell chiming eleven times (I counted) at 4 a.m., to

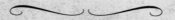

horses' hooves clomping outside the window to our room, to what sounded like three men talking and laughing (all night long and into the morning), to footsteps going all over the entire inn (again, all night long). It was so noisy that I didn't get to sleep until after about 5 a.m., when I finally put cotton in my ears. Then when I fell asleep, I had a terrible dream of a man being hanged right outside the window to our room, which overlooked a courtyard, which I later learned was the site of many hangings.

The next morning I said to the staff, "So, this place is haunted. . . ." They related to me that they've learned to live with the ghosts. They said that they're just playful and noisy spirits, but never hurt anyone. But they also informed me that their other property, called the McLean House, was seriously haunted. That the maids don't even like to go in there, and that often guests leave in the middle of the night.

So, both of these places would seem like great investigations—and you may want to check them out. The McLean House in particular, as it was supposed to be used as a Civil War hospital, and one maid recounted to me that she's had things thrown at her by ghosts, and that she's cleaned the entire house (an eight-hour job) in just under two hours! She said she'd stay in the Talbott Tavern alone anytime overnight, but never at the McLean House. She also said there's a painting of a little boy in particular that seems to change while you look at it.~*Hannah Cwik*

"The minute we turned off the lights in our room, I heard the sound of a door slam shut loudly, a man sneeze, and then loud footsteps going down the hall. . . . I heard all kinds of noises throughout the rest of the inn . . . [from] horses' hooves clomping outside the window to our room, to what sounded like three men talking and laughing. . . . I didn't get to sleep until after about 5 a.m."

STILL STANDING WATCH
AT FORT DONELSON

Fort Donelson on the Cumberland River near Dover, TN, was the site of a Civil War battle that began on February 11, 1862. Although battlefield wags later referred to it as an "exchange of iron Valentines" because much of the fighting took place on February 14, it gave the Union its first major victory in the Civil War, when Brigadier General Simon Bolivar Bruckner surrendered to Brigadier General Ulysses S. Grant on February 16. It also left at least 850 men dead.

In 1867, 670 Union soldiers were buried at nearby Fort Donelson National Cemetery. Fourteen of them were black soldiers from the U.S. Colored Troops, including Reuben Hammond, whose ghost is said to watch over the cemetery now. Both visitors and staff have seen him and he seems friendly, if a little lonely.

⊛ **Fort Donelson National Battlefield: Visitor Center, 120 Fort Donelson Rd., Dover, TN, 37058; Cemetery/ Park headquarters, 174 National Cemetery Rd., Dover, TN 37058, www.nps.gov/fodo/index.htm; open daily 8 a.m.–5 p.m.**

The 1st U.S. Colored Infantry, photographed by Mathew Brady, ca. 1862. By 1865, African Americans made up approximately 10 percent of all Union troops.

A lithograph of the Battle of
Fort Donelson from ca. 1887.

A recent photograph
of the Civil War Altar of
Remembrance at Fort
Donelson Cemetery.

THE BUTCHER SHOP STEAK HOUSE ☞ *Joanne M. Austin*

The Butcher Shop Steak House in Memphis was located in an 1860 building that was rebuilt in 1905 after a fire. During the Civil War, the building had refrigeration, and when Memphis fell to the North in 1862, they stored dead Union soldiers in a cooler in the back. The scene described by Mike McCarthy (www.guerrillamonster.com), a filmmaker who also conducts walking tours, is grisly:

"They crammed so many bodies back there; they were squeezed together and the blood ran down the back of the walls and into Riverside Drive."

That room and the top four floors of the building are no longer in use, although sometimes a candle or light appears in the middle window in the topmost floor, a custom borrowed from Europe during the Civil War to show you had a soldier off at war. Mike recalled a couple on one tour: The woman was trying to get pictures of orbs, and the man stood off to the corner, not saying anything. When Mike explained the theory behind the light, the man said, "That's not why there's a light in the window."

Mike asked if he'd like to tell the group why, and he did. "First of all, a boy or maybe a young man named Jay or James—I can't quite get it—that's the person who was killed in a construction or reconstruction of a building here, and that's the light in the window."

Mike asked, "How do you know that?"

The man said "James" had been talking to him for the last five minutes while he stood on the sidewalk. The group was a little startled, so Mike asked how he heard the voice. The man claimed it was through "radio signals or waves" and that it played out until he couldn't hear them anymore. Then he added, "Before James stopped talking to me, he did tell me that he didn't like you very much!"

Mike laughed at the time, but he made it a point to give a shout to James when he wrapped up at the Butcher Shop because he didn't want anything following him home. [NOTE: The Butcher Shop Steak House's downtown Memphis location has closed since this writing.]

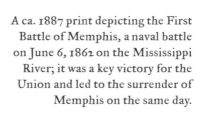

A ca. 1887 print depicting the First Battle of Memphis, a naval battle on June 6, 1862 on the Mississippi River; it was a key victory for the Union and led to the surrender of Memphis on the same day.

Union soldiers drawing water from a well in the South, 1864.

THUNDER HOLE

Just about every town in eastern Tennessee has one: a cave where kids go looking for trouble. In Morristown, it's the Thunder Hole, so called because in bad weather, a frightening roaring or rumbling sound can be heard coming from its entrance shaft of fifty by twenty-five feet.

Local historian Howard Hill claimed that it has a Civil War legend attached to it.

Back in the 1860s, the Widow Cassidy drew her well water from a bucket that extended down into the cave's near-vertical entrance shaft. Her sixteen-year-old son, Massilon, at home on furlough from the Confederate army, heard a detachment of Union soldiers heading their way. Widow Cassidy told Massilon to stand in the bucket and hold onto the rope as she lowered him down into the cave. When the Bluecoats showed up, their captain dismounted and approached the widow, who was still standing by the well.

"Could we have some water for ourselves and our horses?" he asked. She replied, "You're welcome to it, but today's my washday, and I'm anxious to get all my washing done before sundown. So all I ask is that you let me have the first bucketful. After that you can have all the water you want." The captain agreed and waved two of his men over. "Help this kind lady get her bucket up so we can get ours," he said. The men soon raised the bucket containing Private Cassidy. They jumped to grab him, but according to the *Morristown Daily Gazette-Mail*, the captain ordered them to back away, flourished his hat with a bow, and said to the widow, "Madam, the first bucketful is yours, just as I promised."

With that, the Union soldiers quenched their thirsts, watered their horses, then waved good-bye as they set off in the direction of Dandridge.

OLD GREEN (OR YELLOW) EYES

Since the days when Yanks and Rebs fought and killed one another in the woods of Chickamauga and on the steep slopes of Chattanooga, there have been reports of a strange humanoid figure with wild, bloody hair, who's often found lurking around the old battle-fields. Local stories say it is the ghost of a Yankee killed by his Confederate brother, and he's usually referred to as Old Green Eyes or Old Yellow Eyes, though neither nickname is quite accurate. "Old Greenish-Yellow Eyes" seems closer to the color of this specter's glow-in-the-dark optical organs.

He tends to haunt the observation towers that overlook the Civil War battlefields. One of the towers where he has been spotted most frequently is the Wilder Tower just across the state line in Georgia, where they say there are bloodstains on the top four steps that no amount of cleanser can remove.

All we can do, then, is recommend that if you climb up for the view, don't forget to watch your step.

✸ **Lookout Mountain Battlefield Visitor Center at Chickamauga & Chattanooga National Military Park, 110 Point Park Rd., Lookout Mountain, TN 37350, (423) 821-7786, www.nps.gov/chch/index.htm; open 9 a.m.–5 p.m.**

Three soldiers on Lookout Mountain, overlooking Chattanooga, the scene of a fierce battle during the Chattanooga Campaign of October–November 1863.

MINIÉ BALL MIRACLE

The American Civil War has often been called the "first modern war" in part because of the technological advances in warfare—mines, machine guns, submarines, torpedoes, gun turrets, balloons, hand grenades. Despite the advances, the war was wasteful and costly in terms of matériel. For every soldier who was actually hit by a bullet, historians estimate, 240 pounds of gunpowder and 900 pounds of small lead projectiles were used.

The vast majority of those bullets were "minié balls," named for their French inventor, Claude-Etienne Minié. These chunks of molded lead weren't round, but pointed on the front end and hollowed out in the rear so they expanded when the rifle was fired and came spinning out of the barrel like a well-thrown football. Although most missed their target and their range wasn't great, a successful hit was likely to be devastating. The bullets were so big and heavy they left gory, easily infected wounds. They caused more than 90 percent of Civil War battlefield casualties.

It was considered a miracle of the Battle of Chickamauga when Private Edmund Tate survived a shot through the left nipple that went clear through his back. After his companions saw the exit wound, they abandoned him for dead. Lucky for the young private, his brothers returned after the battle subsided to collect his body for burial. The field surgeon was equally astonished: Tate was clearly alive, but the doctor could detect no heartbeat.

The minié ball had created such an intense internal shockwave in Tate's body that it had knocked the heart to the far right side of Tate's chest, where it remained pumping away for the rest of his long life.

A set of deadly minié balls.

Jack Hinson, in an undated photo.

CAPTAIN JACK'S REVENGE

An uninhabited and unpaved dirt road west of Stewart in Houston County, TN, ends at a promontory with an impressive view of Kentucky Lake, the impoundment created in 1944 when the TVA dammed the Tennessee River to control flooding. Before that, this same spot afforded an unobstructed view of the river itself, winding far below the steep bluff where the road ends. This was something that John W. "Captain Jack" Hinson turned to his advantage when he decided that the only manly response he could offer after what had happened to his family was bloody-minded revenge.

Born in North Carolina in 1807, Hinson had settled in this part of the country because it was the kind of place where an independent-minded guy could do what he wanted and be left alone. There were few large plantations, no big towns to speak of, and few industries, so a small-time planter like he was could enjoy a life of hunting, fishing, raising a family, and tending a farm—at that time, the American Dream.

Hinson wasn't completely isolated from the rest of the world, though, and when the states began to quarrel over the issue of slavery, he voted for Lincoln. Within months of the start of the Civil War, this part of Tennessee became a hotbed of guerrilla activity, contested by rival warlords. Both sides included criminals and opportunists all too eager to prey on local folks caught in the middle. Hiding behind their respective "noble causes," thugs from both North and South would kidnap and torture local farmers for money and supplies, then commandeer their property and livestock for their own use.

Perhaps the most hated Union officer in the region was Colonel William W. Lowe of the 5th Iowa Cavalry. Tales of his ruthless approach spread as his men slaughtered livestock, burned houses, wrecked mills, and carried out summary executions. His soldiers dragged two men out of Sunday School at a church just north of Erin, told them to kneel and say their last prayers, and then shot them before they could say "amen." Seven more men were killed in short order, without trial or tribunal.

In the winter of 1862, Jack Hinson's own boys ran afoul of the cruel colonel. They were hunting in the "coaling grounds" between the Tennessee and Cumberland rivers, accused of guerrilla activities because they weren't wearing a uniform (for either side). On Lowe's orders, the two boys were shot by firing squad, their heads mounted on their father's gateposts to serve as gruesome examples of Lowe's command.

Despite his leanings toward the Union, Hinson swore vengeance on the spilled blood of his sons. Taking a specially made seventeen-and-a-half-pound .50-caliber long-range hunting rifle, he left his family, walking into the woods to kill as many Yankees as he could.

Knowing that he could trust no one, Captain Jack entered a self-imposed exile, shunning contact with his home and former neighbors. For years he had hunted through every ridge and hollow of the country between the rivers, and he could silently steal through its forests on even the darkest nights. He knew how to live off the land and kill his own game, carefully retrieving the lead from each deer carcass so he could remold the flattened balls and fire them again. Meanwhile, soldiers began mysteriously disappearing from Forts Henry and Donelson whenever they'd go out on solitary sentry duty, or—if they were on patrol with their platoon— suddenly dropping dead in midsentence, a split-second before the distant crack of that rifle would reach the ears of their comrades.

Hinson's favorite targets, however, were the gun-boats that patrolled the Tennessee River. He lay in wait on a high promontory, hidden behind an out-cropping of rock. Anything in blue was fair game, but officers in particular learned to hide below decks or risk sudden death delivered by the invisible sniper on the ridge above. After each confirmed kill, Hinson carved a small circular mark on the stock of his gun. By war's end there were

thirty-six circles, but historians think he was being conservative, only marking the gun when he was sure he had taken down his prey. Many claim his true toll was more like eighty or a hundred Union soldiers.

Later in the conflict Hinson sometimes served as a scout, guide, or intelligence source for the Confederates. Meanwhile, the Union forces had assigned cavalry and infantry soldiers from nine regiments, along with a specially outfitted team of marines, to hunt down the "one-man battalion" who was now nearly sixty years old. At one point, speaking with Confederate major Charles Anderson, he admitted to finding some satisfaction in his lone quest. "They murdered my boys and may yet kill me," he said, "but the marks on the barrel of my gun will show that I am a long ways ahead in the game now, and am not done yet."

When the war ended, he hung up his rifle (eventually giving it away) and moved to Magnolia, Houston County, to run Magnolia Mill on White Oak Creek with his wife, Elizabeth, until his death in 1874.

There's no plaque or monument to indicate where Hinson carried out most of his self-imposed mission. But not far beyond the end of the road overlooking the water, there's a sudden drop-off, and hidden in the face of the bluff below it is a nearly forgotten outcrop of yellowish strata that old-timers in the area call Name Rock. It's hard to find if you don't know exactly where to look, but if you do, it's easy to see how it got its moniker. Though covered with a skein of names, dates, and initials, it is still possible to discern the oldest marks among them: "Hinson," dated 1863. The "C.S." scrawled before it seems to be a claim of allegiance.

— *Thanks to Chris and Bettie Card*

Background: A drawing of Fort Henry on the Tennessee River by Alfred R. Waud, ca. 1862.

THE PETRIFIED SOLDIER

Of all the graves in the little churchyard that extends to the east of Grassy Cove United Methodist Church, there is one that stands out: a huge, unmarked stone slab resting on a low wall of smaller hewn stones. (All the other burial sites are below ground.) Legend has it that this particular slab once held down the restless remains of what locals called the Petrified Soldier.

He was discovered in a saltpeter cave. Such caves are frequently inhabited by a large colony of bats, whose guano is the source of saltpeter. Saltpeter was used by Native Americans to fertilize their fields and by settlers to make gunpowder. Saltpeter caves traditionally emit a powerful attraction to foolhardy young boys, because there is always the chance of finding old artifacts left behind by Indians, early pioneers, or Civil War soldiers.

A few years after the Civil War ended, local kids ventured into the Grassy Cove Saltpeter Cave, which both Union and Confederate forces had occupied at different points. Lighting their way with pinewood-knot torches, they made their way through the cave's front chambers until they came upon a sight that far exceeded their hopes for cool abandoned booty. On a low platform created by a naturally flat-topped boulder, they discovered a crude stretcher made of hickory bark strips. Upon it lay a soldier in a remarkable state of preservation, fully attired in his gray Confederate uniform. A hat hid his face, but there was no doubt that the man was quite horrifyingly dead. The adventurers scrambled out of the cave as quickly as they could and ran to tell some adults about it. One sent word to the county coroner, James W. "Soup" Matthews.

Matthews and a group of older men reentered the cave and made their way to the primitive bier where they found the dead man. They lifted off the hat and gazed upon a face with eyes closed, as if the man were asleep. He looked to be in his mid-thirties and had mummified to the hardness of rock. There were no visible wounds, lesions, or bruises, and almost no wear on the boots or clothing. It was as if the man had died within days of first putting on his uniform. No autopsy was performed since at that time the law forbade autopsies unless there was sufficient evidence of foul play. In this case there was none.

Eventually he was taken to the old Methodist church in Grassy Cove and lowered into a hole dug in the third grave space to the left of the huge stone slab. Contrary to the legend that grew up later, the unknown soldier's grave was never marked and never under the slab itself.

Within days, people living within earshot of the church began to hear screams at night coming from the churchyard. The doors of the church began slamming repeatedly, and sacramental objects left on the altar would be found dashed to the floor. Then, loud noises began to be heard in the vicinity of the saltpeter cave as well. Children refused to attend the local school since it was so close to the creepy grave. Adults were terrified to walk along Kemmer Road in front of the cemetery after dark.

The soldier was exhumed and moved to an undisclosed cave. Given that caves stay at the same temperature and humidity year-round and that the Petrified Soldier had already mummified, it's likely he's still there today, waiting out eternity in his own private hideaway.

✸ **Grassy Cove United Methodist Church, 262 Kemmer Rd., Crossville, TN 38555**

🖋 "They lifted off the hat and gazed upon a face with eyes closed, as if the man were asleep. He looked to be in his mid-thirties and had mummified to the hardness of rock. There were no visible wounds . . . and almost no wear on the boots or clothing. It was as if the man had died within days of first putting on his uniform."

The cemetery at Grassy Cove United Methodist Church, with the huge stone slab in the foreground.

The bullet-ridden split-fence post from the Officer farmhouse at the Overton County Museum.

OFFICERS' GATE POST

A weather-beaten and lichen-covered chunk of old split-fence post in the Overton County Museum in Livingston, TN, offers stark, if somewhat confusing, evidence about an event that happened long ago in the Sinking Cane (now Rock Springs) community, about three miles north of Monterey.

William and Cynthia Officer were at home on the morning of Saturday, March 12, 1864, serving breakfast to some Confederate officers (including their nineteen-year-old son, John Officer). They were passing the biscuits and retelling the story of the Battle of Stones River that had ended on January 2, 1863, when a company of Union cavalry burst in and killed six of the Confederates in indoor combat. A seventh was dragged out of the house, stood in front of the fence post, and summarily executed by a firing squad. The dozens of bullet holes in the post are presented as evidence that this happened.

As the Yankees were preparing to burn the house, so the story goes, an elderly slave named Abe retrieved his personal belongings, including his old mattress. He came back out with his bedroll, having wrapped the still-alive John Officer inside.

It is a little hard to picture old Abe lugging a mattress containing a nearly grown man inside without raising suspicion. But oral history is, after all, the stuff from which legends are born.

In any case, as it turned out, the house wasn't burned after all. After attempting to set fire to it, the Yankees grew impatient and left.

⊕ **Overton County Museum, 318 W. Broad St., Livingston, TN 38570, (931) 403-0909, www.overtonmuseum.com; open Thurs.–Sat., 10 a.m.–2 p.m. The old Officer homestead is privately owned.**

NATHAN BEDFORD FORREST

Even people who honor the memory of Confederate general and KKK founder Nathan Bedford Forrest find the sculpture south of Nashville on the east side of Interstate 65 between Exits 74 and 80 a challenge to warm up to. Looking like a lunatic, with an oversized head and demonic eyes, the fiberglass figure has attracted more than a few bullets since its unveiling in 1998. But situated where it is, on an island of private land donated by William Dorris to the Sons of Confederate Veterans, and sandwiched between the relentless flow of traffic on the interstate and a busy railroad switchyard, it is almost completely inaccessible.

The equestrian statue of General Nathan Bedford Forrest outside of Nashville by Jack Kershaw.

Before the Civil War, Forrest was a wealthy plantation owner and slave trader. By war's end he was nearly broke but quickly rebuilt his fortune while also helping to found the original Ku Klux Klan. He was the organization's first "grand wizard." Three years later he tried to dissolve it, after becoming concerned about its increasing tendencies toward mob behavior. By then, however, the evil genie was already out of the bottle. The Klan reorganized in 1915 near Stone Mountain, Georgia, and remained a plague for the next seventy years.

Monuments and historical markers celebrate Forrest's wide-ranging escapades in nearly every county in the state. Yet ever since the Confederacy first formed, Tennesseans have always been divided. More than 100,000 Tennessee men joined the Confederate army, more than any other state. At the same time, some 50,000 Tennesseans joined the Union army to fight against the Confederacy. That's more enlistments than about half the states that supported the Union.

Forrest in an undated photo.

REDRUM IN THE READ ROOM

There are two kinds of people who believe in ghosts: those who don't want to run into them, and those who will go to any lengths to encounter them. The front-desk staff at the Sheraton Read House Hotel in Chattanooga are used to dealing with both kinds, for the hotel has a room that is haunted: 311. Some people ask for any room *but* 311, while others beg to be booked into the room on the off chance that the guest ghost will put in an appearance.

The Read House was originally called the Crutchfield House when it opened in 1847. It was occupied by Union soldiers during the Civil War, burned in 1867, reopened as the Read House in 1871, and was rebuilt yet again in 1926. During the yellow fever epidemics of 1873 and 1878, and in the Spanish Flu pandemic of 1918, the hotel served as a hospital. But the ghost of room 311 is neither from the famous nor the ill. According to most accounts she was a "lady of the evening."

The story is that a young Union soldier invited her into the room in 1863. After her "performance," a loud scuffle broke out. The soldier may have been suffering from the Civil War version of post-traumatic stress disorder, or it could be that, as a Southerner, she got in a dispute with him over the war. One story suggests that she wasn't a prostitute but a local woman who fell in love with the soldier and was enraged to discover that he was already married. Whatever happened, the fighting abruptly ended and the next day when the staff went into the room, they found the young

woman dead. Not wanting to rile the population of the occupied city, the army quickly suppressed any mention of the event. The soldier was never court-martialed and the episode was soon forgotten . . . except by the young woman who paid with her life.

The room has been known ever since for unpredictable and sometimes unpleasant events, ranging from relatively innocent nightmares and sudden scalding and freezing water in the bath to more serious matters like luggage being suddenly knocked over and dumped by an unseen hand, laptops and cell phones being swept from desktops and smashed, or even full apparitional appearances by the screaming young woman herself. This time, however, her screams are never heard outside of the room, so if you stay in it yourself, don't expect anyone to come to your rescue if she shows up in full revenge mode.

✹ **Sheraton Read House Hotel,**
827 Broad St., Chattanooga, TN 37402,
(423) 266-4121, www.sheratonreadhouse.com

On the right side of the photograph, behind the Adams Express Company building, is the original Crutchfield house as it stood in 1864.

THE GREAT LOCOMOTIVE CHASE

Almost all the tombstones in the Chattanooga National Cemetery are nearly identical and perfectly aligned, but eight of them curve around a monument topped by a scaled-down bronze locomotive.

The real-life train, the *General*, had been hijacked by the men buried here. The death dates are the same because they were hanged on the same afternoon. And yet they were also the very first recipients of the United States' highest military award, the Medal of Honor. Their story is exciting enough that several movies (including one by Walt Disney) have been based on it.

During the Civil War, the *General* was a prized piece of Confederate railroad equipment. But even more important to the South's war-making abilities was the network of rails that shipped soldiers quickly from one battlefront to another. Because of this, a civilian spy for the Union, Kentuckian James J. Andrews, concocted a daring plan to interrupt Confederate rail traffic by destroying the tracks between Atlanta and Chattanooga. While the *General* paused in what is now Kennesaw, Georgia, to refuel and allow passengers to breakfast, Andrews and his cohorts separated all the passenger cars, hijacked the locomotive, and clipped telegraph lines as the Confederates chased after them with all haste.

A few miles north of Ringgold, Georgia, the *General*, low on fuel and water, blew a valve and lost steam power. The Union raiders jumped off and ran into the nearby woods, but a massive manhunt resulted in their quick capture, trials, and death sentences.

Andrews was hanged on June 7, 1862, in a hasty affair, conducted on a scaffold that was too low to the ground. He died slowly by strangulation. The other members of "Andrews Raiders" were tried in a military court-martial in Knoxville, and seven of them were hanged in Atlanta.

Six members of the group were later the first American soldiers to win the Medal of Honor. But because Andrews and one other man were civilians, they didn't qualify for the award no matter how instrumental they'd been in the attempt to cripple the Confederates. Of the others who participated in the raid, eight escaped and made their way back to the North, and another six became prisoners of war who were eventually traded for Confederate POWs.

The remains of the hanged men were exhumed from their unmarked mass grave and moved to the Chattanooga National Cemetery a number of years after the end of the Civil War.

⊛ **Chattanooga National Cemetery, 1200 Bailey Ave., Chattanooga, TN 37404, (423) 855-6590, www.cem.va.gov/cems/nchp/chattanooga.asp; open Mon.–Fri., 8 a.m.–4:30 p.m.**

The memorial to the Andrews
Raiders in the Chattanooga National
Cemetery, dedicated in 1890.

BEAUTIFUL JIM KEY

Alone gravesite a few miles south of Shelbyville, Bedford County, holds the remains of four individuals: two humans, a dog, and a horse. The horse, equine prodigy Beautiful Jim Key, was a popular entertainer.

No wonder crowds were drawn to him. He could compete in spelling bees, read, sort mail, use a specially adapted cash register to make change, make phone calls, discuss politics, and recite biblical passages entirely from memory. Using numbered and lettered blocks he could add, subtract, and tell time, and by holding a special extended pencil in this mouth he could write intelligible sentences and sign his own name.

Jim was trained by "Dr." William Key, a former slave born in 1833. Bill Key grew up on a farm close to the gravesite, where as a very young boy his phenomenal ability to communicate with animals was recognized. By 1889, when Doc Key found the scraggly, part-crippled colt that he named Jim (after a local drunken stumblebum), he'd been earning a living as a horse whisperer and self-taught veterinarian for more than fifty years. William Key's life story is amazing in its own right—among other things, he had been a double agent during the Civil War, won his freedom in a poker game, took over the farm where he'd previously been a slave and supported his former masters for the rest of their lives, married four times, invented Keystone Liniment, and used its profits to fund his ventures in hotels, racetracks, and restaurants. But it was as the trainer of the little wobbly colt that he gained lasting fame.

Taking the horse with him on travels with his Keystone Medicine Show, Doc Key applied his well-honed skills in training animals "only with kindness, never force or punishment." In 1897 at the Tennessee Centennial Exposition in Nashville, President William McKinley saw Jim and Key perform. McKinley later said that this was not only the most amazing thing he'd seen at the exposition, but among the most astounding phenomena he'd ever seen, period. The notoriety this generated quickly vaulted Jim into stardom and his trainer and their newfound partner, Albert Rogers, into riches. They moved Jim to an estate in New Jersey.

Jim's talents and abilities may have put him in the limelight, but it was his good works that kept him there. He performed repeatedly on behalf of the Humane Society and the Society for the Prevention of Cruelty to Animals. He also broke down color barriers decades before Jesse Owens and Jackie Robinson, since wherever Jim went, his African American trainer went as well, including to command performances for President Teddy Roosevelt. Doc and Jim Key were among the most celebrated acts in the world at the turn of the last century, performing for millions. In the days before TV, this was an amazing accomplishment.

Plagued through his life with joint pains, Beautiful Jim was seventeen when he retired in 1906 to Shelbyville. Dr. William Key died in 1909 at age seventy-six, and Beautiful Jim and his dog-friend Monk both died in 1912. The three of them, together with promoter Albert Rogers, share the grave south of town.

— *Thanks to Mim Eichler Rivas*

✺ **The gravesite is located three miles south of the Shelbyville, TN, courthouse on Hwy. 130 (also known as the Old Tullahoma Hwy.), just west of the intersection of Himesville Rd. and Singleton Rd.**

Opposite, bottom left: A portrait of Dr. William Key from a 1901 performance program pamphlet. During the war, Dr. Key went to Fort Donelson with his master's two sons and protected them during the battle there in February 1862. Afterward, Key continued to assist the rebels while also liaising with the Union and the Underground Railroad. He was captured by the 6th Indiana Regiment and sentenced to hang as a double agent, but won his freedom in a game of poker.

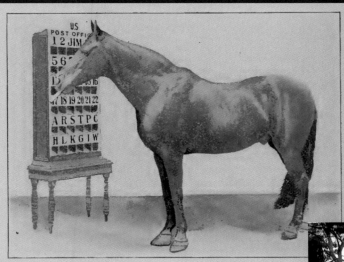

ACTING POSTMASTER.

From the 1901 performance program pamphlet: Beautiful Jim Key sorting mail.

The Bedford County gravesite.

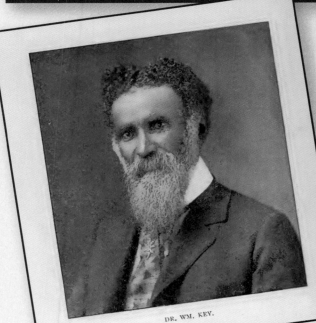

DR. WM. KEY.

PROGRAM.

The audience are requested to ask questions. Please speak distinctly to the horse and he will respond promptly. A hint — he enjoys applause.

1. He opens school. Rings the bell for school to open.
2. Jim picks out any letter, playing card or number asked for.
3. Jim shows his proficiency in figuring, adding, multiplying, dividing and subtracting in any numbers below thirty.
4. He spells any ordinary name asked him.
5. He reads and writes.
6. He goes to the post-office, gets the mail from any box requested, and files the letter in a regular letter file, under any name asked him.
7. Jim distinguishes various pieces of money, and goes to a cash register and rings up any amount asked for, bringing the correct change.
8. Distinguishes colors and flags, and tells the time.
9. Gives quotations from the Bible, where the horse is mentioned, giving chapter and verse.
10. Uses the telephone.
11. Jim takes a silver dollar from the bottom of a glass jar filled with water, without drinking a drop. (Considered one of the greatest feats ever performed by an animal.) Well again.
12. Jim offered for sale. Not wanting to leave, he goes lame. (One of his most amusing and laughable feats.)

6

SINKING OF THE *SULTANA*

In terms of loss of life, neither the *Titanic* or the *Lusitania* sinkings nor the attack on the battleship *Arizona* in Pearl Harbor can top the awful incident on April 27, 1865, just a few miles north of Memphis. The steam packet *Sultana* was overloaded with thousands of passengers when its boilers exploded. In the mayhem that followed, 1,547 people reportedly died (the actual number is believed to be closer to 1,800) and nearly 500 were severely injured.

The *Sultana* was among the most modern Mississippi riverboats of its day. Only two years old, it was 260 feet long and 42 feet wide, but had a draft so shallow that it could still operate on only three feet of water. Two steam engines, powered by four high-pressure boilers, could deliver twice as much steam using half as much coal as conventional boilers. Its thirty-one wood-paneled staterooms were among the largest of any boat on the river. Outfitted with carpeting and crystal chandeliers, on a typical run the *Sultana* could accommodate seventy-six passengers in private rooms and up to three hundred deck passengers, plus a crew of eighty and up to 660 tons of freight.

On that particular day, however, the *Sultana* was carrying far more than an ordinary load. Under the command of Captain Cass Mason, the *Sultana* was traveling from New Orleans with a normal-capacity load. But in Vicksburg, Mississippi, thousands of haggard, malnourished Union soldiers—most of them just released from hellish POW camps such as Andersonville—lined the banks of the river, desperate to get back home to the North. Dozens of steamboats like the Sultana jammed the riverfront, each hoping to cash in on the sudden demand for transport by charging higher than their standard rates for deck space. Greed led many of the boat captains to succumb to a kind of feeding frenzy, agreeing to take on far more than their usual number of passengers. By the time the *Sultana* pulled away from the Vicksburg docks, more than 2,300 people were jammed on board a vessel with only seventy-six life preservers and one lifeboat, all of them intending to go at least as far as Cairo, Illinois.

When the *Sultana* reached Memphis, some cargo was unloaded and the vessel was refueled. Just before midnight that evening, it departed the docks in the midst of a major thunderstorm. Due to the rain, the river was higher than usual, but the *Sultana*'s engines were powerful, and despite its load it made headway against the strong currents. But then around 2 a.m. the next morning, after passing Paddy's Hen and Chickens (a string of little islands now consolidated as Chicken Island, or Island No. 42–45), first one and then two more of the four boilers exploded.

The blast destroyed the bulkhead supporting the main deck as it ruptured the furnaces beneath the boilers, simultaneously heaving tons of embers, red-hot firebricks, and body parts high into the ☞

☞ "For weeks afterwards, the Mississippi below Memphis was strewn along its shore with stark, mangled bodies, lodged in the crotches of trees, [or] caught horribly in the undergrowth of willows and cottonwoods."

The last and possibly only existing photograph of the crowded, ill-fated steamboat *Sultana* on the Mississippi River the day before her boilers exploded and she sank on April 27, 1865.

A *Harper's Weekly* illustration from the May 20, 1865, issue, depicting the explosion of the *Sultana*.

air while dumping hundreds of other bodies directly into the flames. Scalding steam shot through the passageways and filled the main cabins. Amid screams, the boiler deck sagged and caved in, and the twin smokestacks towering over the superstructure began to totter and fall.

Survivors of the initial explosions jumped into the frigid river. Over the next hour or so, the *Sultana* burned and sank as other survivors managed to cling to bits of wreckage and float down the river or were rescued by other riverboats. One Union soldier later told of how, after he finally washed ashore in Arkansas, he passed out, only to wake up many hours later covered in a dry rebel uniform. He never found out who the compassionate Samaritan was. Others said that when they jumped into the river to escape the flames, their biggest fear was that the pet alligator on board had gotten out of his pen and was now somewhere in the water among them.

Most of those who were aboard the *Sultana* that day didn't survive to tell such stories. "For weeks afterwards," one witness recalled, "the Mississippi below Memphis was strewn along its shore with stark, mangled bodies, lodged in the crotches of trees,

[or] caught horribly in the undergrowth of willows and cottonwoods."

What caused the disaster? No one knows for sure. Some blamed hasty repairs done in Vicksburg, some attributed it to the incredible overloading, and some pointed to the ship's tubular boiler design, which was still new and prone to building up internal deposits of dried silt residue when the muddy river water was converted to steam. One final possibility was sabotage. Former Confederate agent Robert Louden bragged on his deathbed that he had used a bomb disguised as a lump of coal to blow up the boat, though few historians credit his claim.

Despite the magnitude of the disaster, the sinking of the *Sultana* soon slipped from the public consciousness. In fact, no one knew where the wreck of the *Sultana* itself was until 1982, when Memphis attorney Jerry Potter finally located what remained of the ship buried fifteen feet below a soybean field a mile and a half from the river. A monument was erected in Memphis's Elmwood Cemetery in 1989, near the three unmarked graves of some of the victims.

⊛ **Elmwood Cemetery, 824 S. Dudley St., Memphis TN 38104, (901) 774-3212, www.elmwoodcemetery.org**

THE DASHING ASSASSIN'S MUMMY

ntil 1923, the garage behind a house located at 1234 Harbert Street in Memphis sheltered a mysterious lodger who, in fact, had been dead for some twenty years. The house's owner, prominent Memphis attorney Finis L. Bates, decided not to bury the poor fellow because he needed him as a witness. Only he, Bates believed, could substantiate a strange claim that he was none other than John Wilkes Booth, the actor who assassinated President Abraham Lincoln on April 14, 1865.

On April 26, twelve days after the assassination, Union cavalry tracked Booth and a fellow conspirator to a farm near Port Royal Crossroads where they holed up in a tobacco barn. Booth's comrade surrendered, but Booth refused to come out, so the soldiers set fire to the barn. Booth was shot in the neck, and soldiers dragged him from the burning building. They laid him on the farmhouse porch, where he died three hours later.

The corpse was taken back to Washington for autopsy and identification and then buried inside a warehouse storage room. Several years later, the bones were moved to an unmarked grave in Baltimore.

All of this was smoke and mirrors, according to Bates, who claimed that a man who looked similar to Booth was killed at that northern Virginia farm. Bates held that Booth had escaped and made his way to Texas, where he spent the next thirty-five years 🖛

A studio portrait of John Wilkes Booth, ca. 1860–65.

A photograph of Finis L. Bates from his book, *Escape and Suicide of John Wilkes Booth.*

F. L. BATES, Author.

living under the adopted name of John St. Helen, then David George. According to Bates, the real John Wilkes Booth died of arsenic poisoning after a drinking binge in Enid, Oklahoma, in 1903.

Bates befriended John St. Helen in 1872, when Bates had a law practice in the same town where St. Helen established a reputation as a gifted speaker. Following an 1876 incident, St. Helen thought he was dying and confessed to Bates that he was really John Wilkes Booth. He told Bates how he escaped, and how the soldiers killed the wrong man. Then he handed the lawyer a photo of himself, asking Bates to send it to his brother, the actor Edwin Booth, who would want to know of his death. St. Helen recovered, but Bates never forgot the confession. He kept in touch with St. Helen and years later, when he learned his old friend had really died, he went to Enid to claim the body.

When he arrived, he found that the undertaker had embalmed but not buried the corpse, since St. Helen died without leaving a will or money for a funeral. Bates paid the embalming bill and took the corpse of his old pal back to Memphis. Meanwhile, the arsenic that St. Helen swallowed combined with the embalming fluid and the hot dry air of central Oklahoma to mummify the body.

After spending much time and money trying to prove that St. Helen was indeed Booth, Bates published *The Escape and Suicide of John Wilkes Booth, or The First True Account of Lincoln's Assassination, Containing a Complete Confession by Booth Many Years After His Crime* in 1907. To promote the book's release, Bates took the mummy on tour (shown here), and it became a grisly sideshow feature at carnivals and fairs for several years. The book went through multiple printings before the sensation died down.

Bates hoped that the book and the mummy exhibition would encourage the army to reopen the

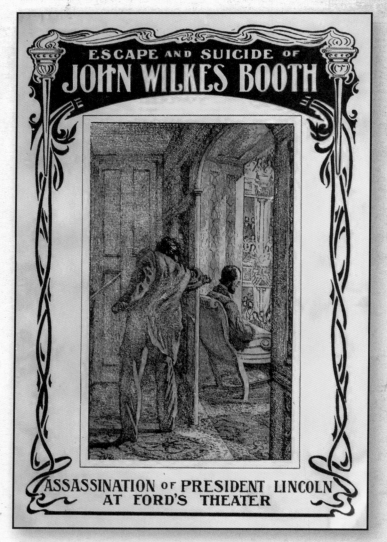

The cover of Bates's book, published in 1907.

☛ "According to Bates, the real John Wilkes Booth died of arsenic poisoning after a drinking binge in Enid, Oklahoma, in 1903."

case, but it never happened. After Bates's death, a 1924 *Harper's* magazine article created a national sensation, and the mummy went back on the sideshow circuit. After that, the corpse was bought and sold by several amusement operators, kidnapped and held for ransom, seized as collateral for a bad debt, and featured in Jay Gould's Million-Dollar Circus in the late 1930s before appearing in *Life* magazine in 1944.

In 1931 Chicago radiologist Orlando Scott x-rayed the mummy. The corpse had a fractured left fibula, a disjointed right thumb, a scarred eyebrow, and a scarred neck—all of which matched descriptions of Booth's injuries. The X-rays also revealed an object in the mummy's stomach which, when they cut into the body to retrieve it, turned out to be a signet ring with the letter *B*. This gave rise to a theory that Booth swallowed his ring during his escape to destroy evidence of his identity.

Did John Wilkes Booth ever reside in Memphis? All anyone can say for sure is that some mummy did, for the evidence seems to have vanished. The last time the location of the mummy was officially documented was in 1942, when it belonged to John Harkin, the Tattooed Man in the Hagenbeck-Wallace Circus.

Chicago radiologist Orlando Scott posing with the mummy, ca. 1931.

DE SOTO WAS HERE

Just across the street from the now-defunct Marine Hospital on Metal Museum Drive in Memphis are two ancient earthworks (now called the Desoto Mounds in Chickasaw Heritage Park) that may have been used as temples honoring the river or the sun. According to legend, the largest, Chisca Mound, is said to be the place from which Spanish explorer Hernando de Soto and his men first laid eyes on the Mississippi River in 1541.

The Spaniards didn't stay for long. As soon as they could build rafts and float across the river, they left. De Soto died of a fever the following year without ever having found what he was looking for: gold.

More than two and a half centuries later, Fort Pike was built here, taking advantage of the mounds' elevation for observation posts. From 1814 to 1818 they were the site of the Chickasaw Indian Agency, and during the Civil War they were incorporated into Fort Pickering and used as Confederate cannon emplacements. Chisca Mound was hollowed out and used to store gunpowder in 1863.

✸ **Chickasaw Heritage Park is located between Riverside Dr. and Metal Museum Dr., Memphis, TN 38106**

A bunker in one of the mounds at Chickasaw Heritage Park.

PERPETUAL MOTION OF JACKSON'S WHEEL

Before the Civil War, Confederate inventor Asa Jackson had hit upon the solution to a problem that even the Renaissance master Leonardo da Vinci himself had failed to solve. Using simple carpenter's tools, and perhaps inspired by the biblical description of a vision in Ezekiel 1:16, the Tennessean from Lebanon built a machine that could generate its own impetus. In other words, he had found the secret to "perpetual motion." Once it began to turn, the wheel-within-a-wheel would turn itself by itself until its parts physically wore out. That was the concept, anyway.

Jackson, born in 1792, was already sixty-nine when the Civil War began. During the hostilities he feared his invention would fall into enemy hands, so he took it apart and hid it in a cave. Even without Jackson's epoch-making device, the Union won anyway. Jackson retrieved his contraption, put it back together, and set it in motion long enough for witnesses to vouch that it worked. It ran, they said, for many days, perhaps weeks, before Jackson stopped it. Satisfied that he'd made his point well enough, he removed some of the key pieces and left it that way. Four years later he was dead.

Since then, no one has been able to figure out how the detached parts fit back together or how to make it run again. The weird mechanism sits in a case by itself in John Rice Irwin's Museum of Appalachia, in Norris, tantalizingly daring some other brilliant soul to come along and solve its puzzle. This could be your ticket to the Nobel Prize in physics.

✳ **Museum of Appalachia, 2819 Andersonville Hwy., Clinton, TN 37716, (865) 494-7680, www.museumofappalachia.org. Hours and days vary with the seasons; consult the website.**

Asa Jackson's perpetual motion wheel on display at the Museum of Appalachia.

Bottom: Cumberland Presbyterian Church in Greeneville, TN, with an arrow pointing to where the cannonball is lodged in the wall; *right*: a close-up view of the cannonball.

CANNONBALL CHURCH

Greeneville's Cumberland Presbyterian Church was built just as the Civil War began. Four years later a skirmish broke out in the streets surrounding it as Union cavalry raided the town on September 4, 1864. During the fight, former cannabis farmer and disgraced Confederate general John Hunt Morgan hid in stables on the ground floor of the church (the sanctuary is upstairs) and then tried to make a break for it. He was shot in the back and killed just across the street when he refused to halt after being ordered to do so by Private Andrew J. Campbell of the 13th Tennessee Cavalry, who had been on the Confederate side earlier in the war—an irony, since Morgan had begun the war as a Lincoln supporter. A small stray cannonball, fired during the scuffle, lodged in the bricks in the front of the new church. Rather than remove it, the congregation chose to let it stay there as a reminder of the incident.

✺ **Greeneville Cumberland Presbyterian Church, 201 N. Main St., Greeneville, TN 37745, (423) 638-4119, www.gcpchurch.org**

LITTLE LIL

James Gaines, a Knoxvillian, betrothed Belle Porter of Ohio shortly before the Civil War broke out. The war, of course, separated them when their families wound up on opposite sides. James rose to the rank of colonel in the Confederate army and lost an arm just before the conflict ended. Realizing that things might have changed since their engagement was announced, he offered to release Belle from their commitment if she were now turned off by his "mutilation and poverty." Belle married him anyway.

Lillien, the youngest of their three children, died of an illness at age seven, not long after they returned to Knoxville. She was buried in the Old Gray Cemetery in Knoxville. Nowadays, both mourners of young children and star-crossed lovers often leave tokens of loss and affection in the little girl's lap.

✷ **Old Gray Cemetery,**
543 N. Broadway, Knoxville,
TN 37917, (865) 522-1424,
www.oldgraycemetery.org

Toys are left for Lillien Gaines on the statue of her gravesite at the Old Gray Cemetery.

CHAPTER FOUR

LOUISIANA

SO-LOW OF WILSON POINT ROAD

Wilson Point Road in Rapides Parish, LA, fizzles out into a driveway leading to the last house twenty miles southeast of Pineville. Southeast of that is an enclave surrounded on three sides by the Red River, effectively cut off from the rest of the state. Highway 1 may be only a mile across the river as the crow flies, but it takes almost half an hour to get there by car. And back when roads weren't paved and cars traveled at slower speeds, it could take almost half a day. As one elderly resident put it, "We was so far from everything out here no one could even hear us if we screamed." Screaming, in fact, would probably have only made matters worse, since the bow in the river that loops around the point is famous for its echo, and your screams would only have been joined by others sounding just like yours.

Living in this isolated enclave meant that whenever problems came along, locals were forced to face them alone. One such problem: a particularly pesky phantom hell-bent on terrorizing the community. The consensus on the ghost's identity is that in life he was a Confederate soldier who returned home after fighting on the losing side in the Civil War. Most of the Wilson Point folks were former slaves from the nearby Grimes and Wilson plantations who had intermarried with Native Americans and, learning of the great emancipation, weren't about to revert to subjugation. Upon returning home, the soldier tried to order the liberated slaves back to the fields. They responded by attacking him and then stringing him up on a nearby tree limb.

Whether because of the soldier's rage or the collective guilt of the murderers, his spirit grew restless. Before long, his vengeful ghost returned and began regularly pestering the community from beyond his shallow, unmarked grave. And over time, locals have learned that there is only one way to deal with the spiteful spirit—be prepared.

SHAPE-SHIFTER SHENANIGANS

Old So-Low, as locals call him, is a shape-shifter and dealing with his antics can be tricky. In a July 1982 article in *Alexandria Town Talk*, ninety-year-old Rollie Lipscomb told about his first after-dark encounter with the ghost more than forty years earlier. So-Low suddenly appeared on a sandy path as Lipscomb and his wife were coming home from visiting a sick friend.

> I heard something fall out of a tree like a sack of dirt into the water. I says . . . "Old feller, don't start nothing." Something with horns like a billy goat appeared in the road. His eyes looked like balls o' fire. . . . I then stepped aside and let him pass. He had martingales on, just like a little dog. . . . He was grunting with every jump he made. . . . I ain't never seen nothing like that in my life.

So-Low's antics were unpredictable. The ghost didn't merely jump out of the bushes or run down the path. Instead he was often seen dragging heavy objects like washtubs or pieces of furniture through the woods. The furniture left long gouges in the soft ground, but no accompanying footprints were ever found. Locals soon took to carrying stout clubs to fend So-Low off at night, and although no one was ever physically harmed, the spirit's spiteful acts certainly made life more frustrating.

Previous pages: The ironclad USS *Essex* at Baton Rouge, LA, 1862.

"Others met old So-Low in every shape, fashion, or form that he can be met," said Lipscomb, although in the late 1940s, after automobiles started rumbling down the country lanes, the sightings waned. Still, Lipscomb was convinced that "So-Low is still out there somewhere—waiting." The ghost has also appeared as a bright light moving through the trees and as a shadowy figure easily detected by dogs or horses but difficult for people to see. Once in a while, if it's still early enough in the evening, blood is visible on the ghost's neck where presumably the martingale collar had cut into him.

✸ **Wilson Point Rd., Rapides Parish, LA: take Harris Ferry Rd. west off Highway 454, a few miles south of Ruby; turn left onto Wilson Point Rd., which forks south.**

"I heard something fall out of a tree like a sack of dirt into the water. I says . . . 'Old feller, don't start nothing.' Something with horns like a billy goat appeared in the road. His eyes looked like balls o' fire."

FRONT AND CENTER

Front Street in downtown Natchitoches is a pretty happening place when it comes to paranormal activity. According to *Old Natchitoches Parish Magazine*, town residents report seeing a man dressed in Civil War clothing wandering around the area in the evening after the shops close. Some say he's decked out in a Confederate uniform, but according to local legend he's a Yankee—Brevet Brigadier General Napoleon McLaughlin, who was gunned down on Front Street around 1872. The problem with this theory is that McLaughlin did survive his wounds and lived until 1887.

McLaughlin was part of the Union occupation forces left behind to keep local citizenry under control after the war ended. The West-Kimbrel gang, run by Confederate veterans John West and Laws Kimbrell, had set itself up as a group of insurgent warlords in the largely lawless country just across the Red River from Natchitoches. McLaughlin had been sent from Washington with express orders to bring the gang under control.

According to historian Jack Peeples, McLaughlin's techniques were brave but also somewhat simpleminded. After one of his officers was killed by a member of the West-Kimbrel gang, the relatively inexperienced general took only an orderly and set out on a search-and-destroy mission without any other backup. He crossed the river and rode up to the Kimbrel house and dismounted. He knocked on the door and Ma Kimbrel stepped out. When McLaughlin asked her where the boys were, she lied, saying they had fled to Texas.

On the way back to Natchitoches, McLaughlin ran into Billy Kimbrel. The general shot him down during the ensuing gunfight. According to legend, McLaughlin

A stretch of Front Street in Natchitoches.

decided to make an example out of Billy by dragging his corpse to Ma Kimbrel's house and draping it over the fence alongside her drying laundry. Some time later, General McLaughlin was strolling along Front Street when he was struck by a single gunshot fired from the darkness. No one knows whether it was Billy's brother Laws Kimbrel, another member of the gang, or even Ma Kimbrel—whose infamous bloodlust rivaled that of her sons—who fired the shot. And no one really knows who the Front Street ghost really is—could it be Billy?

LOYD'S HALL OF HAUNTS

William Loyd has been his own worst enemy since birth, which by now must be at least a couple of centuries ago. According to legend, as a young man in England he was considered such a scoundrel that his family disowned him. He was forced to drop one of the *L*s in his last name to further disassociate him from the rest of the Lloyds and then was told to leave England entirely.

Being a rogue of low morals and high aspirations, he naturally headed to Louisiana, where he bought a three-thousand-acre parcel of land on Bayou Boeuf near Cheneyville, in Rapides Parish, built a house there sometime between 1816 and 1830, and then set himself up as a planter. The local Indian tribes apparently thought even less of him than his former relatives did, as a couple of flint arrowheads found embedded in the front door of the house seem to attest. As one of his neighbors quipped, "If you'd ordered a wagon train full of rascals but all you got was Bill Loyd, you'd still think you'd got your money's worth."

By 1864, when the Civil War had reached this part of Rapides Parish, wily "Grandpa Loyd" was considered (or else pretended to be) too old and too feeble to fight and chose to sit out the war at home. He invited Union troops to camp on his land and then wined and dined the officers. He may have hoped to curry a few more favors (or at least save his house from being burned down) by offering to tell them where the rebel forces were hiding.

But if trying to stay on the winning side was his goal, this time it backfired. Following his directions, ☞

☞ **"If you'd ordered a wagon train full of rascals but all you got was Bill Loyd, you'd still think you'd got your money's worth."**

Loyd Hall,
photographed ca. 2009.

the Union soldiers walked straight into a rebel ambush. Unfortunately for Loyd, enough of them managed to escape and straggle back to their campsite at his plantation to point an accusing finger in his direction. Justice was swift. Loyd was dragged out of his house, dipped in boiling tar, and then hanged from one of the oaks in his own front yard. That oak stood until 1957, when Hurricane Audrey finally uprooted it.

PLANTATION PHANTOMS

A poltergeist that's frequently plagued William Loyd's house and property ever since has been attributed to the man's violent (and perhaps unjust?) death. Rearranging or hiding silverware, ringing doorbells, banging on walls and the piano, knocking pots off the stove, tipping over heavy furniture and slamming doors, the spirit seems forever bent on deviltry, much as Loyd himself had been during his lifetime.

Loyd is by no means the only one to have died on the property. According to family oral history, a few days following Loyd's summary execution a young Yankee soldier, in love with one of the young women in Loyd's household, deserted and stayed behind when his fellow troops pulled up their tent stakes to begin the Red River Campaign. He hid in a small storage closet under the roof off the east room on the third floor. When he finally emerged, he accidentally surprised (or enraged) Loyd's widow, who stabbed or shot him and then left him to slowly bleed to death on the floor, where bloodstains marking the scene of the incident supposedly come back even after the floor is cleaned. Unable to lug him downstairs by herself, Loyd's widow tipped his body out a third-floor window and then dragged his corpse into a shallow grave beneath the house.

Another bloodstain marks the spot where William Loyd's niece Inez, jilted at the altar on her wedding day, slashed her wrists and bled to death. Here again, however, the orally transmitted stories vary in the details, since some of the versions insist instead that she jumped to her death through that very same third-floor window, only to be impaled on a big shard of glass when she hit the ground below. Or could this have been the fate of Annie Loyd, yet another niece? Since all the records were destroyed during the Civil War, the various tales and legends about the house and its occupants have become entangled in the turbulent years that followed. Although they do all agree on one thing: Several restless spirits occupy the plantation.

Since the Civil War, more than a dozen families attempted to live in the house. But whether driven out by ghosts or daunted by both the ever-advancing decay of the structure and its remote location, none managed to stay for very long. Misfortune and suffering seemed to grip anyone who tried to live there, but each new owner had to discover the curse for himself and then keep it a secret, lest he be unable to resell it to the next unsuspecting buyer.

HARMLESS HAUNTS

The old Loyd property changed hands again and again, shrinking from 3,000 to only 640 acres as the forlorn mansion gradually became so overgrown with vegetation that when Virginia Fitzgerald and her husband bought the property in 1948, they had no idea it included the old house. Pulling down the vines that

The bloodstain on the floor of the third-floor east room of Loyd Hall—color enhanced—photographed ca. 2009 before the house was remodeled as a B & B.

thickly shrouded it, the Fitzgeralds rediscovered the ten-room Georgian manor; cleaning out decades of debris revealed its "floating" staircase of tiger maple and the beautifully intricate plasterwork of its sixteen-foot ceilings. Confident that they had found a treasure, the Fitzgeralds and their young children moved in as soon as the rooms were cleared and the broken windowpanes replaced. They had not, however, counted on sharing the house with its long-term residents or heard about the ongoing curse; so when tragedy struck, they were unprepared. Within months of moving in, both Mr. Fitzgerald and his daughter were killed in a mysterious accident.

Undaunted by the supernatural, Virginia Fitzgerald chose to remain in the house. Determined to somehow carve out a place for the living among the spirits of the dead, she furnished the place with antiques—including a massive 1878 piano that once belonged to politician William Jennings Bryan and that is still in the house today—and began delving into its past. Some things, like the bullets she found embedded in the stairs, never yielded an explanation, but in time she came to terms with the phantoms. Her surviving son raised a family there, and eventually her grandchildren learned to play with one of the ghosts, "Harry Henry," as they called the lovelorn young soldier. Harry entertained them with violin music he played on the broad second-floor veranda and often wandered through the house in his old Union uniform. He and Inez, and another spirit the family called Sally (thought to be a former slave), all seemed to be harmless, even benevolent toward the Fitzgeralds, who had lived in the North before buying the property. But William Loyd apparently never forgave the Union for the tarring and hanging and never ceased his troublemaking until the living Fitzgeralds finally moved out of the mansion into a cozier modern cottage they built nearby.

Loyd's Hall is now a bed and breakfast and event space. If you choose to stay there, we recommend you keep quiet about where you're from—if you hail from the South, Harry might not like it, and if you say you're from up North, you might have William to deal with. So mum's the word either way.

⊛ **Loyd Hall Plantation, 292 Loyd Bridge Rd.,**
Cheneyville, LA 71325, (318)776-5641, www.loydhall.com

The Battle of Mansfield depicted in an engraving from *Frank Leslie's Illustrated Newspaper*, May 14, 1864.

KEACHI COLLEGE

Fieldwork in search of the weird can sometimes be confusing. Depending on which map you consult, a town in western DeSoto Parish can be spelled Keatchie, Keatchi, Keitche, or Keachi, and pronounced either KEE-chee or key-CHAI. In any case, the town itself, while only a ghostly shadow of its former self, is a charming collection of old buildings, many of which are now listed on the National Register of Historic Places.

There's also a one-story school on the site of the former Baptist Union Female College (also called the Keatchie Female College, Keachie Women's Academy, or Keachi College), organized in 1856 or 1857 to offer the maid of arts and mistress of English degrees to women seeking higher education. The college had barely begun awarding diplomas to its first graduates when the Civil War began.

During and after the Battle of Mansfield (also known as the Battle of Sabine Crossroads) on April 8, 1864, and the Battle of Pleasant Hill the following day, the college was requisitioned as a Confederate hospital. Army surgeons performed unmedicated amputations, resulting in wagonloads of arms and legs to be hauled off and buried. A large hole was dug in the side yard for burying buckets of soldiers' blood, and a morgue was set up on the school's second floor.

According to eyewitnesses, the smell of "seared flesh, clotted blood, splintered limbs, and dismembered corpses" filled the air. The wounded were "sickening ☛

Opposite: The abandoned site of the former Keachi College.

"Despite years of scrubbing
and repainting,
students continued to complain
they heard screams,
saw pooled blood
dripping down the stairs."

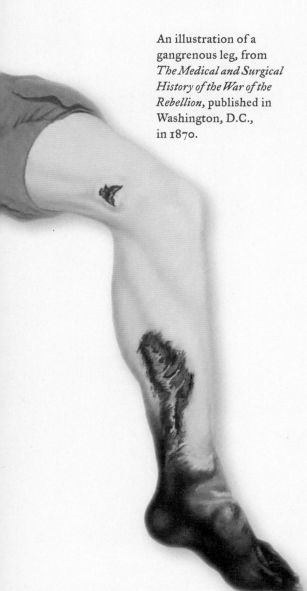

An illustration of a gangrenous leg, from *The Medical and Surgical History of the War of the Rebellion*, published in Washington, D.C., in 1870.

sights. Some shot in the face, both eyes out, head bent, arms, legs, everywhere." Describing a similar scene in Pleasant Hill, historian Vicki Betts remarked on "how numbed the children came to be at the sight of the dead soldiers, so much so that some were caught jumping from body to body and crowing like roosters."

For local people such as Lafayette Price, the horror had only begun when the fighting ended, for the dead were buried in mass graves. According to Price, "They just dig a big hole and put 'em in and threw dirt on 'em. I went back after two or three days, and the bodies done swell and crack the ground. The dead of both armies were laid head to foot and the whole hillside was wrapped up with soldiers and the unburied dead. When the earth began to warm later in the season, huge cracks appeared in the ground. It swelled up in ridges, like a big mole run, and the entire hillside turned green with flies."

The largest Civil War battle west of the Mississippi also turned out to be the last major rebel victory; both students and townsfolk were left psychologically and physically scarred for years. Alums of Keachi would recall for decades afterward the screams of the wounded soldiers as young women frantically shredded and scraped towels and linens to make "lint" for stanching blood or making disposable bedding, while inscriptions gouged into walls by the wounded and dying remained visible as long as the building stood. Despite years of scrubbing and repainting, students continued to complain they heard screams, saw pooled blood dripping down the stairs, and smelled cauterized blood vessels and the stench of gangrenous flesh.

In 1879 the school began admitting male students, but they too were troubled by the horrible groans and strangled cries of wounded and dying soldiers. Not long after Louisiana College opened in Pineville in 1906, Keachi College closed, then burned to the ground. When a new school opened on the same site, pupils dreamed of men in bloodstained uniforms.

Now the place is abandoned, except for the occasional black snake slithering through heaps of fallen lumber or gaping holes in the floor, and the birds that have built nests under the eaves. During the day, that is. At night, it's a whole different story.

Houmas House, now a historic museum; events are held on the surrounding plantation grounds and its buildings.

HAUNTED HOUMAS HOUSE ☞ *Fiona Broome*

At Houmas House in Darrow, LA, the dead walk in plain sight among the living. From the majestic front gates to the cupola on top, this pre–Civil War mansion hosts ghosts who act as if they have every right to be there. Between its grand, turbulent history and its wide array of daytime ghosts, the house isn't just the "crown jewel of River Road," but a rich, profoundly haunted site for ghost hunters.

Built by Alexander Latil in the late eighteenth century on land purchased from Houma Indians, ownership of the aptly named Houmas House changed many times over the last two hundred years. In 1825, Colonel John Preston acquired the property and expanded the original four-room house to accommodate his growing family. Colonel Preston, his wife, and their eight children spent many happy years at the house and then tragedy struck—one of the young girls passed away suddenly. Soon after, the grieving family moved to South Carolina and never returned.

The home's next owner was Irish immigrant John Burnside, who in 1857 tripled the size of the Houmas House plantation lands to more than 300,000 acres, becoming the largest sugar planter in the South. Claiming British citizenship—Ireland was part of Great Britain in the 1860s—Burnside protected Houmas House from attack during the Civil War as Union soldiers burned many neighboring plantations. Burnside died a bachelor, and the house passed to Colonel William Porcher Miles, a statesman and a Civil War legend who created the Confederate battle flag (the ubiquitous Confederate flag adopted in 1863, even though it was overlooked in favor of the "Stars and Bars" in 1861). Colonel Miles also lost a young daughter at Houmas House; she died unexpectedly at age seven and was buried in the family cemetery, in sight of ☞

William Porcher
Miles, ca. 1859.

the plantation home. However, in 1927 the Mississippi flooded its banks and displaced all the coffins in the family plot, dragging them to the river's watery depths. None of the bodies were ever recovered.

Since then, Houmas House has been as famous for its ghosts as for its magnificent antebellum architecture, furnishings, and gardens. The home's elegant and eerie setting may be why Hollywood producers filmed the classic 1964 horror movie *Hush . . . Hush, Sweet Charlotte* there. Enthralled by the ghostly legends surrounding this estate, the movie's star, Bette Davis, slept in Houmas House's most haunted room.

GHOULS AT THE GATE

I had a few otherworldly encounters of my own at Houmas House. The morning after an overnight stay at the house as part of a public relations tour, I saw a stout ghoul walking ahead of me. I followed him up a steep flight of stairs to the widow's walk, but I had to be mindful of my own steps and saw only his black, polished boots and crisp navy blue trousers a few feet in front of me. When I reached the widow's walk,

I circled a few times looking around for the man, and was surprised to find that I was alone.

The stocky ghost has also been spotted standing at the railing atop Houmas House. He may be John Burnside, looking for Yankee ships on the river. However, some say the man is in uniform, and thus more likely to be Colonels Preston or Miles. This ghost appears at dawn, but he is also seen as late as 11 a.m., and again around dusk.

In addition to the stout ghoul, the ghost of a tall, slender black man may greet you at the historic main gate of Houmas House. Clad in simple, dark clothing and described as well over six feet tall, the ghost is always seen pacing—back and forth, over and over again—as if waiting for someone. I myself saw him as I looked down from the widow's walk encircling the house's cupola. He looked up at me, paused, nodded, and then resumed pacing at the gate. If he hadn't simply vanished after a few minutes, I'd have thought he was another visitor, or someone who worked at the house. The tall, pacing man can be seen in a picture displayed at Houmas House and some say his ghost appeared briefly in *Hush . . . Hush, Sweet Charlotte*.

APPARITIONS EVERYWHERE

If you tour the house, especially on foggy or rainy days, look out the windows on the upper floors. From there, you may see the shadowy outlines of Civil War soldiers gazing toward Houmas House. Approximately 260,000 Confederate soldiers died defending the flag that Colonel Miles created, and this historic connection may be why Houmas House's ghostly activity increases around April 9, the anniversary of the Confederate army surrender. The soldiers are most often reported outside the fence, along the road by the river.

Some visitors sense ghosts in the oldest part of Houmas House. Latil's original eighteenth-century home—now the rear wing of the mansion—has been converted into a gourmet restaurant, Latil's Landing Restaurant. Café Burnside, another eatery on the property, was once part of a cotton warehouse. Today, visitors sip mint juleps and remark about "something odd"—and perhaps ghostly—overhead. Nearby, especially around dusk, look for a ghostly figure at the doorway of Houmas House's wine cellars. At one time a water cistern, the building was recently converted to a home for fine *spirits*—more than a thousand cases of red and white wines.

✳ **Houmas House, 40136 Hwy. 942, River Rd., Darrow, LA 70725, (225) 473-9380, www.houmashouse.com. Tours are given daily; ghost enthusiasts should visit late in the week or during the weekend, when the site is open until 8 p.m.**

A railing of the upstairs porch at Houmas House, where ghostly apparitions have been seen.

THE GHOSTLY GIRL

The room in which Bette Davis stayed was once used as a nursery. Over the years, visitors to the Houmas House have reported seeing the ghost of a little girl appear as a reflection in the mirror or glass surfaces around the room and claim that the apparition disappeared when they tried to look at it directly. The ghostly girl, described as being less than five feet tall with shoulder-length light brown or dark blond hair, has also been spotted (and photographed) on a staircase that adjoins the room. In 2003, sightings of the little girl spiked when the current owner, Kevin Kelly, began restoring the house. On many occasions, workmen on site reported seeing a little girl playing on the freestanding staircase at the end of a first-floor hall. Witnesses say the young ghost wears a dark, old-fashioned dress and hides one of her arms, as if trying to conceal a disfigurement. Nevertheless, those who have encountered her claim she is a cheerful and pleasant entity. Who is this young spirit? Some say she is the ghost of John Preston's daughter, while others believe the apparition is of William Porcher Miles's young girl. No one knows for sure.

OLD STATE CAPITOL: THE HAUNTED CASTLE

Some buildings seem to cry out that they're haunted. Outfitted with turrets, towers, creepy corridors, weirdly sweeping staircases, heavily paneled doors that creak on their hinges, stained-glass windows that turn ordinary daylight into crepuscular gloom, they almost seem to scream, "Haunt me, baby! Haunt me bad!" Every town should have at least one such place—some old pile of overblown architecture that makes you want to whistle out of sheer nervousness when you hustle quickly past it at night.

Louisiana's Old State Capitol in Baton Rouge is just such a place. From a distance it looks like something a kid might build on the beach, but up close it looms threateningly high, with crenellated medieval towers and crossbow slits that bring Robin Hood and the Sheriff of Nottingham to mind. Mark Twain considered it the ugliest building on the Mississippi, referring to it as "a little sham castle" and a "pathetic architectural falsehood" and even suggested that it should have been dynamited to put it out of its misery.

We couldn't disagree more. As aficionados of the weird, we think the Old State Capitol is coolness incarnate.

THE SPECTRAL SENATOR

Not only does the Old State Capitol cry out as a hometown haunt, but it actually delivers the ghoulish goods. What's more, the ghost doing the haunting has been identified as Pierre Couvillon, who served as a state representative and senator from Avoyelles Parish from 1834 until 1851. He would likely have remained in government longer, but he died of an apoplectic fit after uncovering yet another layer of corruption among

An illustration of Union troops hoisting the U.S. flag on top of the Baton Rouge capitol, May 7, 1862, from *Frank Leslie's Illustrated Newspaper*; the building was used as a Union prison and garrison until the accidental fire of December 28, 1862.

The dramatic facade of the Old State Capitol in Baton Rouge, lit up at night.

demoted to a civic activity space and allowed to slump into poorly maintained drabness that barely hinted at its former government grandeur. But finally in the 1980s and early 1990s, a major restoration effort reinvigorated the building's magnificence and, at the same time, possibly reawakened its resident ghost. Pierre was back, and he was excited to be a part of it all again.

Before long, security officers started filing reports of alarms going off and motion sensors registering the presence of moving objects during nights when the building had been securely locked down. Tools and small items left in locked rooms began mysteriously disappearing and then reappearing in other parts of the building. Video cameras revealed nothing, but eventually footprints were discovered when some maintenance work in one chamber (the former state senate) had left a fine powdering of plaster dust on the polished floor. The prints led directly to the former desk (surmounted by his portrait) of Senator Couvillon. That was enough proof to make believers out of the Old State Capitol staff.

Rather than call for an exorcist to rid the building of its spectral senator once and for all, they took the opposite approach and decided to capitalize on it. Nowadays, brochures call attention to the cathedral-like interior dome of the main hall, point out the fossils in the marble flooring, describe the intricate brass hardware on all the doors . . . and encourage visitors to keep a sharp lookout for Pierre, the Capitol ghost.

his fellow lawmakers. Unusual for the Robin Hood–like stance he maintained among his colleagues, Couvillon was apparently outraged by how other wealthy politicians used the privileges of their office to further enrich themselves. During one of his angry outbursts at this perpetual state of affairs, he fell dead.

But maybe Couvillon never left office. Even during the twenty long years between 1862, when Yankee troops accidentally set fire to the building and left it a smoking ruin, and 1882, when repairs and restorations finally began, his tall, glaring figure was sometimes spotted wandering among the blackened walls, keeping an eye on things. When the building reopened to government activity in the 1880s, Pierre was among the members of the senate, sometimes casting a vote from beyond the grave (a time-honored Louisiana tradition). Dead or not, he remained a regular attendee until Governor Huey Long's skyscraping New State Capitol opened in 1932 and the legislature moved to the north end of downtown Baton Rouge, leaving Pierre behind in the little castle.

For a long while, it seemed as if Pierre had vanished from the scene for good. The old Gothic building was

⊛ **Louisiana's Old State Capitol, 100 North Blvd., Baton Rouge, LA 70801, (225) 342-0500, http://louisianaoldstatecapitol.org; open Tues.–Sat., 9 a.m.–4 p.m.**

UNCLE TOM'S CABIN

One of the greatest Lost Imaginary Historical Sites of Louisiana has to be Uncle Tom's cabin. Until not so long ago, tourists driving between Alexandria and Shreveport would stop at Little Eva Plantation near Chopin to take pictures of an old shack identified as the very last cabin where the kindly old slave had lived out the last years of his wretched life. After reverently soaking in the historical impact of the decrepit hut, visitors could walk up a hill to frown at the grave of the infamous Simon Legree. A few steps further brought them to a fenced-in area where they could gaze solemnly at the actual grave of Uncle Tom, the slave that Legree had mistreated. In fact, Legree was so cruel that when Harriet Beecher Stowe described the racial situation in her 1852 novel *Uncle Tom's Cabin, or Life Among the Lowly*, the book's release became one of the pivotal events leading up to the Civil War.

The only problem is that Stowe never visited Louisiana. In 1853, she wrote a follow-up to her novel, called *A Key to Uncle Tom's Cabin*, in which she made it clear that the plantation described in the book was based on one she'd visited in Kentucky, and Uncle Tom was a character based on a composite of many stories she'd heard about slavery since her childhood. But never mind; the tourists needed to see the cabin so they could take pictures of it, and there one stood in Chopin.

But it was more artificial than they realized. Built in 1959, the cabin was made to *look* old, and a few steamy Louisiana summers also weathered it nicely.

✱ **The grounds of the former plantation are now private property.**

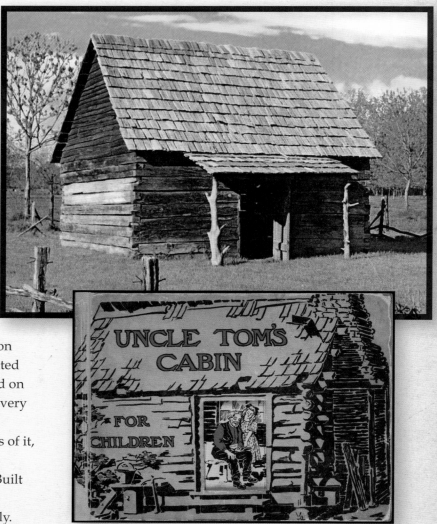

The faux Uncle Tom's cabin on the Little Eva Plantation.

The cover of a children's edition of *Uncle Tom's Cabin*, ca. 1908.

THE STOWAWAY

Discovering the secret shadows of a place you thought you knew is frightening. It's like finding out that the friendly guy at the bakery moonlights as a serial killer or that your kindly old aunt is involved in a drug ring.

Stow's Bar in Ruston was a bit like that. The ground floor of the old place was one of those beer dives with graffiti and pool tables that some folks call colorful or seedy, but not scary. The upper floors of the same building were less predictable, cold and foreboding even on a sultry day. Behind a locked door and a steep flight of worn wooden steps is a former boardinghouse, hotel, home for the elderly, and clinic. Before that, according to what we heard, it was a Confederate hospital.

Plenty of evidence to support all these uses is scattered throughout those floors, including sagging beds, piles of old magazines, boxes of cotton batting that rats have taken up residence in, and, in one room, an abandoned operating table.

We met a guy who said he'd tried to spend a night upstairs and then changed his mind. "I realized I wasn't alone," he said, ". . . my girlfriend and I heard something scraping, and then some footsteps just like somebody was walking toward us down the hall. But I flashed my light down that way and didn't see nothing! I told Carla we should get out of there, and I acted like I was doing it for her sake, but the truth was I was probably more afraid than she was. I thought all those stories about the upstairs at Stow's was just a joke, but after that, I didn't think so anymore. There's something up there. Not just birds, but something big and heavy enough to make the boards creak."

✳ **Stow's Bar is now closed.**

"I realized I wasn't alone. . . . my girlfriend and I heard something scraping, and then some footsteps just like somebody was walking toward us down the hall. But I flashed my light down that way and didn't see nothing!"

A photograph of the decayed upstairs of the former Stow's Bar in Ruston, LA, believed to be the former site of a Confederate hospital.

→ CHAPTER ←
FIVE

MARYLAND

THE GHOST OF BIG LIZ

Marshes provide some of the most fertile land imaginable for growing legends. Something about misty, flat, sparsely populated land that's perilous to walk through at night spawns the creepiest legends. And that's exactly what happened in Dorchester County with the legend of Big Liz. She's sometimes called Bigg Lizz, as if six letters are simply not enough to describe this big-boned woman from the Delmarva Peninsula.

Liz was a large and muscular slave who came to an unfortunate end at the hands of her master. Some versions of the story are set during the Revolutionary War, while others say it happened during the Civil War. There's no definitive version of the tale, and although the events in most of the stories are the same, the significance of the story is quite different depending on how it is told. Whichever account you prefer, there's no solid historical evidence to back it up. We'll stick to the Civil War version of the story here, and follow it up with another example set in the Revolutionary War.

A certain plantation owner was a member of the army of the Confederate States of America, and President Jefferson Davis made him responsible for a substantial war chest. Around that time, he discovered that one of his slaves was acting as a spy for the Union. He well knew the punishment for treason and dreaded what might happen if his household would be found responsible for it. So he determined to put a permanent stop to the security risk, which meant putting a permanent stop to the life of the slave in question. She was much too big for him to handle by himself,

so he had her drag the war chest out into the swamp and dig a hole for it. She worked for hours at the task, until she was too exhausted to defend herself. At that point, her master drew a sword and beheaded her. Her body fell on top of the chest in the hole, and he covered it up with the freshly dug swamp dirt. Only when he was finished did he realize that he had buried only her body. Her head had rolled off and was lost. He assumed that wild animals would deal with it, and that as a traitor, she deserved no better.

The following day his body was discovered lying on the ground beneath his bedroom window with a look of horror on his face. Some believed that the ghost of the woman he had killed rose from the grave, found her head, and came after the man responsible. Now, they say, she still roams around the area by night, making sure that nobody touches the gold in the chest. She paid with her own life for the right to keep it, and nobody's going to take it away from her in death.

✳ **Blackwater National Wildlife Refuge Visitor Center, 2145 Key Wallace Dr., Cambridge, MD 21613, (410) 228-2677 (Visitor Center) or (410) 228-2692 (Refuge Office), www.fws.gov/blackwater**

An artist's interpretive rendering of Big Liz.

Previous pages: Private Soldier Monument, Antietam National Battlefield, photographed by Carol M. Highsmith, ca. 1980.

The Big Liz Revolution

Just outside of Cambridge lies
the Greenbriar Swamp. Around the start of the Revolutionary War, the Bucktown Plantation lay on the outskirts of the swamp, owned by a greedy slave driver whose name is lost to history. He was afraid that his money would be stolen by British soldiers, so he hatched a plan to keep the bulk of it safe. He put gold in a chest and took it into the swampland with one of his strongest slaves, a huge woman named Big Liz. He commanded her to dig the hole, and watched her do it as he sat back and ate his lunch. When she was done, he commanded her to put the chest in the hole. While she was distracted at this task, he took a yard-long tobacco knife and swung it towards Big Liz, slicing her head clean off.

He buried her body on top of the chest, at one stroke ensuring that the secret location of the chest was safe, and turning the place into a grave to deter anyone who might be digging in the area anyway. But his plan backfired. He served in the army during the war, and boasted about his plan to his fellow soldiers. And after he died in battle, some tried to look for the chest. But everyone who did try backed off when they visited the Greenbriar Swamp. By night, they could hear howling from the undergrowth. Some people say they could see a large headless figure wandering around with something tucked under her arm, something that turned out to be her head. ~ *Brendan*

Summoning Big Liz

There's a local legend you hear
at scout camp and other places that you can call up the spirit of Big Liz. You drive up to the cemetery and flash your lights three times over the graves, honk your horn three times, and shout out her name three times. You reverse out and drive to the bridge. With your front tires on the bridge, you do the same thing: Flash, honk, and call out three times. Then you roll down the windows, cut the engine, and wait.

If it works, they say the wind will pick up and you'll hear a gate open. You may see a light coming towards you across the marsh.

The light will take the shape of a large headless woman. You'd better hope you don't look like Big Liz's master, because she's had hundreds of years to get even and she may try to turn your car over and kill you. This has never worked for me, but it may be because I picked the wrong cemetery. There are three of them around Cambridge, all of them old, so it's not clear which is the right one. ~ *Shelley*

An eerie photograph of Blackwater National Wildlife Refuge in Dorchester County, MD, where Greenbriar Swamp is located . . . and where the ghost of Big Liz may still roam.

"Sickles was our kind of war hero. He boxed up his broken limb and mailed it to the newly formed Army Medical Museum with a card that read, 'With the compliments of Major General D.E.S.'"

Major General Daniel Sickles poses for a portrait after his leg was amputated, along with four members of his staff, by Mathew Brady, ca. 1863.

MORE MACABRE MEDICINE

On the second day of fighting at the battle of Gettysburg, the commander of the 3rd Army Corps, Major General Daniel Sickles, lost his leg. A twelve-pound cannonball shattered his shinbone, and because the overworked field hospitals lacked the time and facilities for delicate surgery, his only option was amputation. On July 2, 1863, General Sickles's right leg was cut off just above the knee.

But Sickles was our kind of war hero. He boxed up his broken limb and mailed it to the newly formed Army Medical Museum with a card that read, "With the compliments of Major General D.E.S." The following year, on the anniversary of his loss, the general went to visit his leg at the museum. He repeated the pilgrimage every July 2 from then until his death.

Now you can do the same thing too. The Army Medical Museum has grown from its origins as a collection of "specimens of morbid anatomy" and "projectiles and foreign bodies removed" into a full-fledged

General Sickles's right lower leg bones and a cannonball similar to the one that caused the wound, in the collection of the National Museum of Health and Medicine.

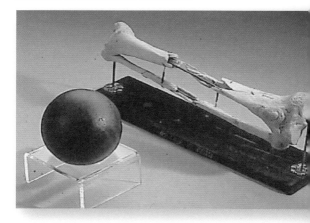

multimedia educational establishment called the National Museum of Health and Medicine.

But despite the noble moniker and its prestigious address in the Walter Reed Army Medical Center in Washington, DC, the museum still has its roots firmly grounded in morbid anatomy and health problems that have concerned armies since time immemorial—from shattered bones to diseases we don't talk about in polite society. There are certainly plenty of educational exhibits suitable for school field trips here, of course, but there's also a collection of medical oddities that's as macabre as anything we at Weird have ever seen.

This is the museum that the essayist Sarah Vowell visited during her Assassination Vacation tour to view the bullet that killed Abraham Lincoln. It is on display alongside fragments of the president's bone and hair, and the bloodstained cuff of the museum's representative at the autopsy. In short, this is a morbid tourist's dream spot.

As we have traveled through the state collecting stories, we've heard that the museum has toned down its exhibits quite a bit over the past few decades. Old-timers still reminisce about going there as a rite of passage, because only real men and women could handle the sights on display. All we can say is that it must have been really grim back then, because it's not for the faint of heart (or stomach) now.

✸ **National Museum of Health and Medicine, 2500 Linden Ln., Silver Spring, MD 20910, (301) 319-3300, www.medicalmuseum.mil. Open 364 days a year, 10 a.m.–5:30 p.m. (closed Christmas Day); adult visitors must present photographic ID.**

LEECHES

The museum also features some real live examples of that staple of ancient medicine, leeches. Because an excess of blood was once believed to be the cause of a host of medical problems, leeches were applied to adjust the fluid levels. They not only suck out excess blood to control bleeding, but their saliva acts as a blood thinner. One delightful fact on display is that these nasty little bloodsuckers are back in use in some hospitals. Unfortunately, they don't say which hospitals they are, or we'd know which ones to avoid. And then, of course, there are the things floating in jars, magnified to unnatural size by the glass and liquid they're in. By the time of the Civil War, the use of leeches was not as widespread (but maggots were used for the first time during the war as therapy to clean out rotting tissue). In any case, the less said about both, the sooner we can go and get lunch.

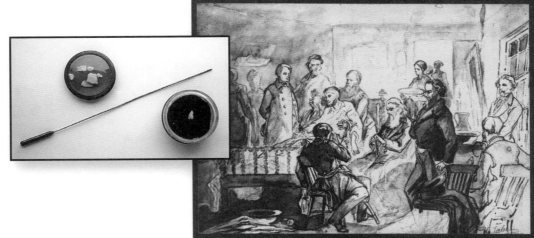

Far right: Sketch of Abraham Lincoln's deathbed scene by Hermann Faber, Army Medical Museum illustrator, 1865; *inset*, the probe used by Dr. Barnes to locate the ball and fragments of Lincoln's skull from the autopsy.

OLD SOLDIERS NEVER DIE.
LIKEWISE, AIRMEN AND SAILORS?

With Maryland's pivotal position near the centers of government during the War of Independence and its strategic position during the Civil War, this state has seen a lot of war. And to anyone with a bent for the paranormal, that means there's a strong possibility that some military ghosts still walk the earth here. Point Lookout is one of the thousands of places where old members of the armed forces continue to march the earth.

✳ **Point Lookout State Park and Civil War Museum, 11175 Point Lookout Rd., Scotland, MD 20687, (301) 872-5688, www.civilwar.org/civil-war-discovery-trail/sites/point-lookout-state-park-and-civil-war-museum.html and dnr2.maryland.gov/publiclands/Pages/southern/pointlookout.aspx. The park is open daily 6:00 a.m.–sunset; call for museum hours.**

Fort Lincoln during the Civil War.

A lithograph of Point Lookout from 1864, showing a view of Hammond General Hospital to the left and Camp Hoffman, the tragically overcrowded prisoner-of-war camp. The hospital closed in 1865 and the buildings were demolished.

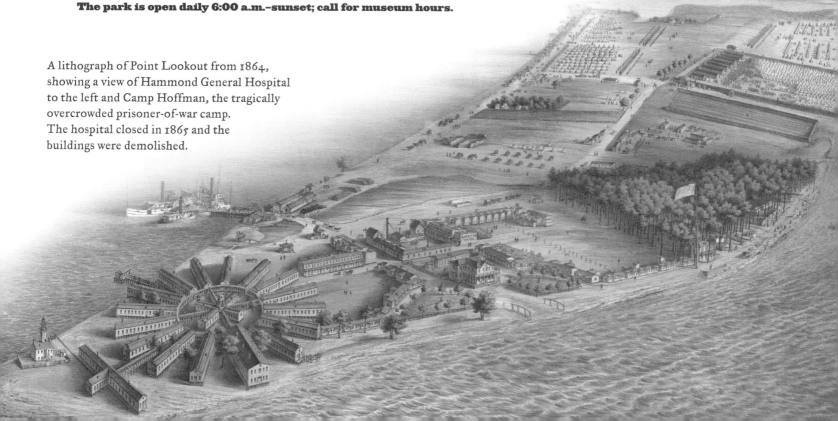

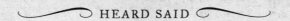

Lookout, It's Smallpox?

At the southernmost tip of Saint Mary's County, at the convergence of the Potomac River and the Chesapeake Bay, lies Point Lookout State Park. Mention this area to any local and talk of the paranormal will result. The area has a tragic history. In the 1600s, when the first settlers arrived, an entire family was killed at the point by Indians. In 1860, a lighthouse was built, which is often called the most haunted in the world. In 1862, the Government started a hospital to treat wounded Civil War soldiers and shortly after, a prisoner of war camp was opened with room for 10,000 Confederates. It ended up housing 20,000. Next a smallpox hospital was established. All in all, about 4,000 people total lost their lives on the point, and about 3,000 are still buried there in unmarked graves. Ghost stories are rampant, but the weirdest was when a wall in the lighthouse glowed green for ten minutes. That's pretty darn weird! ~*Sean Myers*

It Wasn't Me!?

One night last fall, a few of us amateur ghost hunters went out for a drive to Point Lookout at the southernmost point of Maryland. It is a very scenic ride with a lot of straight and curvy roads for us to enjoy. We arrived at the park around 11 p.m.; it's open 24 hours because of the night fishermen on the piers. Fort Lincoln is still there: It's the main fort that was on the peninsula. It was a Union prison and hospital for the Confederate soldiers. At one point, there were supposedly 10,000 soldiers there. Many who died were buried in unmarked mass graves.

So we pull in and pay and head down to where the lighthouse is. The lighthouse is very old and supposedly very haunted as well. It's right on the very end of the peninsula. It was very dark and very windy and we could feel the mist from the Chesapeake's choppy waters. My wife got cold and wanted to go back to the car, so I said I'd walk her back. Now our five-month-old Chihuahua, Thor, seemed to be very uneasy in this area, not wanting to leave Alicia's side and seeming to sense something in the direction of the water.

I left the two of them in the car and began walking back to the group that had slowly walked down to the restroom area. When I got down to them, my friend Evan said, "It took you forever to walk down here!" I looked at him, very puzzled, and said, "I just started walking down here 15 seconds ago." Evan looked at me like I was crazy.

He said he saw the outline of a tall figure walking very slowly in the dark from the lighthouse to where they were all standing about three to four minutes before I walked down to them. The individual seemed to be in no hurry to get anywhere. No one else besides us was out at the lighthouse area.

As soon as Evan and I realized that it wasn't me he saw, we all split up real quick and had a quick look around. Nothing. We got back to the car and my wife hadn't seen anything, but the dog was still very, very antsy. I have done some searching on the Net and found out that others have had similar experiences, with some even getting close enough to make out the Confederate uniforms. Others will see whole brigades march across the road in their rearview mirror, only to turn around and see nothing. To this day, we're not 100 percent sure of what Evan saw. You can draw your own conclusions—I know I have. ~ *thestereogod*

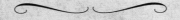

GATHLAND PARK'S SPOOK HILL

Gathland State Park, on the outskirts of Burkittsville, was the site of the Civil War battle for Crampton's Gap, which took place on September 14, 1862. There is a War Correspondents Memorial Arch on the site that commemorates journalists who lost their lives in the Civil War, but there's a more surreal experience to be had in the area. There is a slope in the park called Spook Hill, and it's one of the nation's famous antigravity spots. As the story goes, you can set your car in neutral on this slope and feel yourself rolling uphill instead of downhill.

There have been many explanations for this phenomenon. One is that the whole thing is an optical illusion. The road only appears to slope upward because of the grade of the surrounding terrain. In fact, you're just rolling downhill, and the weird feeling you get when it's happening is disorientation between what your eyes and your sense of balance are telling your brain. Another explanation is that the area is one of those spots where gravity doesn't drag you down normally: Something at the top of the slope has a greater gravitational pull than the entire mass of the planet at the bottom of the slope. A third explanation for the phenomenon is a lot creepier but more in keeping with the area's history.

The Battle at Crampton's Gap was a decisive one in the Civil War, and the Confederate forces did not come off well in it. They were outnumbered six to one and lost almost nine hundred men. This was the first Union victory against Lee's armies and was a direct antecedent of the bloodbath at Antietam three days later. It's not a happy place for the South. And the sheer volume of Confederate dead led to some pretty unpleasant tales of mass interment.

In one account, the Confederate army, in its rush to get to Antietam, paid a local man named Wise to bury fifty of the dead soldiers' bodies. He dumped the bodies in a well, they say, and began to see apparitions of one of the dead men shortly afterward. Eventually, he had to remove all the bodies and bury them properly in shallow graves. The notion was that when the South won the war, the bodies would be exhumed and given a place of honor somewhere special like Arlington National Cemetery. In fact, they were exhumed six years later to be reinterred in the Washington Confederate Cemetery.

But around that time, people began hearing ghostly voices in the homes and the tannery in Burkittsville. They still say the site of the old tannery is haunted, and any car parked there overnight may have marks on it the following day from soldiers' boots. It's said the antigravity effect of the hill is caused by the ghosts of Confederate soldiers, struggling to get their cannons into position at the top of the hill and win the battle.

✹ **Gathland State Park, 900 Arnoldstown Rd., Jefferson, MD 21755, (301) 791-4767, http://dnr2.maryland.gov/publiclands/Pages/western/gathland.aspx; open sunrise to sunset.**

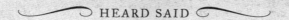
Spook Hill's Hoofprints of Gravity

Near Frederick is a hill called Spook Hill, which supposedly contains Civil War tunnels. If you drive up this hill and put your car into neutral, it will go up by itself. If you sprinkle some powder on top of your car, you will find hoof prints in the powder from a local ghostly horseman. Spook Hill is actually located just outside of Burkittsville. From Harpers Ferry, take Route 340 toward Frederick, and take the third exit over the Maryland bridge. Turn left off the exit ramp and drive six miles to Burkittsville. At the square in Burkittsville, turn left again, and drive half a mile to the town limits. You will see a barn on the left. Slowly drive up the hill where, at the top, you will see several historical markers on either side of the road. ~*Anonymous*

Brother Against Brother in Finzel Cemetery

This story unfolds in the town of Finzel, which is located north of Allegany County. The town has one road, with the old Finzel cemetery located at the end of it on the outskirts of town. During the Civil War, two brothers took up arms on opposing sides—talk about a family feud! One brother fought for the South and the other brother fought for the North; both fought tirelessly. Nonetheless, the two brothers met often in secret inside the small, secluded graveyard to discuss the war and to catch up on stories about the family and various goings-on. However, late one night the brothers got into a heated argument in the cemetery. Having broached the dangerous topic of politics, they argued about which side was morally right. It was an argument that ended tragically. Push led to shove, which led to concussion when one of the men fell and hit his head on a tombstone. The Northern brother, who lay bleeding and begging God for his life, looked into the eyes of his Confederate brother and told him that he would remain there and await his brother's return with help. He told him they could later finish the battle to see who was correct. The Southern brother ran off, presumably to summon assistance. Whether he just kept going, or met some unexpected fate, no one knows, but the help never arrived and the Yankee brother died.

People say that to this day he is still waiting in the cemetery for his brother to return. Witnesses report that if you walk to the rear of the cemetery, near the largest headstone, you may come eye-to-eye with the baleful stare of the now long-gone Union soldier. ~*Beverly Litsinger, MarylandGhosts.zoomshare.com*

CEDAR HILL CEMETERY: LOST AND FOUND ☞ *Brian Goodman*

Following the railroad tracks out of Havre de Grace toward the Susquehanna River, you come to a patch of wooded scrub on a dead-end road called Elizabeth Street. Beneath the leaves and brush lies a missing piece of Havre de Grace history: Cedar Hill Cemetery, a final resting place of Civil War veterans, nameless vagabonds, and the victim of a bloody murder more than one hundred and fifty years ago.

A short scramble up a grassy hill and into a thick scrub of woods and weeds, a deer trail leads first to a simple gravestone in the ground and then to about a dozen more, but only a handful remain standing and fewer still are legible.

Some slate stones have survived the weathering of the last century and look as if they could have been carved a year ago and not 150 years ago. A heart-shaped stone once sat awkwardly tilted, but now rests beneath soil and brush—much like the occupant of the grave.

One stone is eerily engraved with the Latin phrase *Mori Vincent Omnes*, which means "Death Conquers All."

Another headstone bears the name of a Mary Elizabeth who died on August 21, 1874, at the age of only three months and four days. Eight headstones have some kind of markings on them, and a half-dozen more are just crumbling stone. Most unsettling is evidence of more graves in the numerous sunken pits on the property, indicative of collapsed coffins.

While most of the tombstones have toppled or crumbled with time and weather, the government-issued headstones of two Civil War veterans remain standing and contain valuable information that answers some questions, but asks volumes more.

One of the soldiers seems to have lived the simple life of a musician and shoemaker before dying of consumption in 1871; his story is modest when compared to that of his comrade resting a few feet away.

The Cedar Hill Cemetery lies in the woods near the railroad tracks of the Amtrak Susquehanna River Bridge in Havre de Grace.

Born in Ireland, Casper Smith enlisted and became a private in Company H, 2nd Regiment Eastern Shore, Maryland Volunteer Infantry. His first brush with death occurred on July 18, 1864, during a battle at Snickers Ford in Virginia, where he was shot in the lower abdomen. Amazingly, Smith survived the gunshot wound, only to die nearly two decades later, the victim of a sinister plan and a vicious crime. The January 13, 1882, edition of the *Aegis and Intelligencer*, an ancestor of today's *Aegis* newspaper, trumpeted the deed in its headline, "Horrible Murder of Havre de Grace Captain."

On Christmas Eve 1881, Captain Smith left Havre de Grace aboard the schooner *Shelldrake*, which carried guano to Baltimore. The ship was expected to arrive back in Havre de Grace on December 28 but on December 31, Richard Moore, a deckhand on the *Shelldrake*, returned to the city alone, without the schooner or Smith.

When the owner of the ship went to Baltimore to investigate the disappearance of the *Shelldrake* and its crew, a grisly scene awaited him. The ship was found docked and covered in snow, which indicated it had not been moved or tended to recently. Smith was found dead, facedown with holes in his temple, bloody handkerchiefs stuffed in his mouth as a gag, and two small kegs of powder—perhaps to blow up the ship and destroy evidence of the gruesome murder.

It was determined that the death blow came from an iron marlinespike, a pointed hand tool used to separate strands of rope, and was delivered by Moore. Moore, who at the time lived with his mother and three brothers in Havre de Grace, was arrested and convicted of second-degree murder, for which he was sentenced to eighteen years in a penitentiary.

Captain Smith, who during the war had taken a gunshot to the stomach and lived to tell about it, was dead at the age of forty-five at the hands of his own deckhand. Now Smith lies forgotten on the wooded hill.

The cemetery is believed to have opened in 1838 and was abandoned only a decade later, but there are stories that, even as late as the turn of the twentieth century, it was still being used as a paupers' plot. It disappeared from city maps after 1945 and at present doesn't show up in any city land or tax records.

Few ever set foot these days on the once sacred soil, leaving the dead alone with quite a view over the living below.

Two of Cedar Hill Cemetery's surviving slate gravestones: baby Mary Elizabeth's, *top*, and the stone of Captain Casper Smith, *bottom*, whose gruesome death in 1882 was front-page news in Maryland.

SPIRITS OF ANTIETAM ☞ *Troy Taylor*

Of all the Civil War sites where the dead are said to walk, none are as haunted as the battlefields. It was on these fields where men fought, lived, died, suffered, screamed, and bled—and where, most likely, they left a little piece of themselves behind. On the battlefields are the spirits of the past.

On the far western edge of Maryland is the Antietam Battlefield, found just outside of the small town of Sharpsburg. Perhaps the best preserved of all of the sites the National Park Service administers as National Battlefields, it looks much as it did at the time of the battle in 1862. On a clear day, when a crisp wind is blowing across the grass, you can almost imagine yourself in another time. You feel that if you looked up, you might actually catch a glimpse of a weary soldier, trudging on toward either death or victory.

The Battle of Antietam took place on September 17, 1862. It would become known as the bloodiest single day of the entire war, with combined casualties of 23,100 wounded, missing, and dead. The battle itself was considered a draw, but the effect on both sides was staggering. The wounded were left behind at places like the Lutheran Church in Sharpsburg, a house west of the town of Mt. Airy, and at Grove Farm, which President Lincoln visited after the battle. It has been said that the floorboards in this house are still stained with the blood of those who fell, and that more than 140 years later these stains can't be sanded or scrubbed away.

Many other tales still linger about the battle, and some people believe that the soldiers—and the aftermath of the deeds committed here—may linger too. ☞

Opposite: Rows of statues at Antietam National Battlefield, photographed by Carol M. Highsmith, ca. 1980.

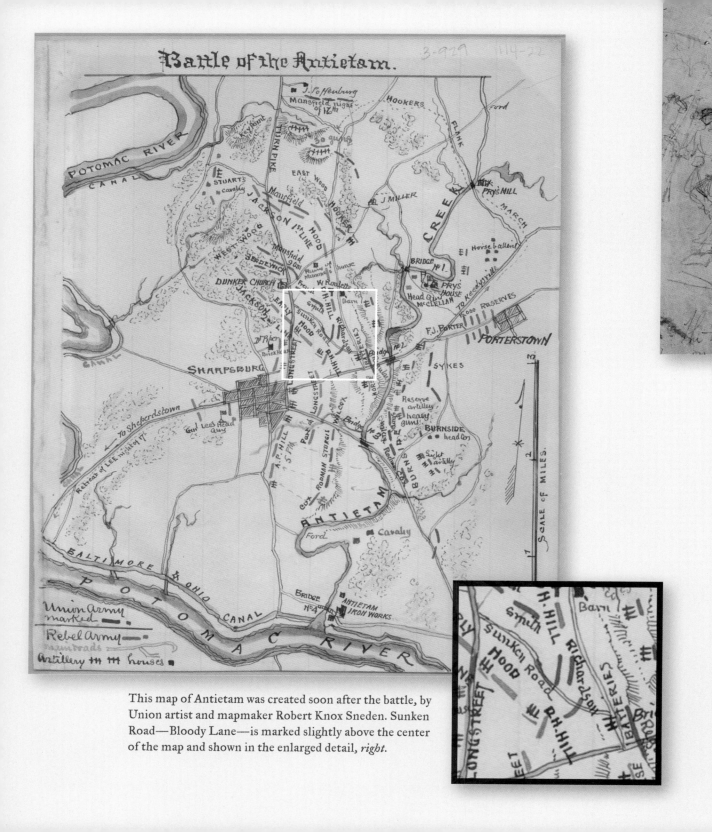

Battle of the Antietam.

3-929 114-22

This map of Antietam was created soon after the battle, by Union artist and mapmaker Robert Knox Sneden. Sunken Road—Bloody Lane—is marked slightly above the center of the map and shown in the enlarged detail, *right*.

A sketch of the Irish Brigade created on the scene during the heat of battle by Irishman Arthur Lumley, a Special Artist attached to the Union army.

"FAUGH-A-BALLAUGH!"

The battle at Antietam was centered in the middle of General Lee's line, at a sunken country road dividing the fields of two farmers. Lee ordered the center of the line to be held at all costs. On the day of the battle, the road served as a rifle pit for two Confederate brigades. Union troops approached within yards of the road before being fired on. The Union commander fell at once and his men wavered and then retreated, only to charge the Confederate line five more times.

The Federals repeatedly tried to overrun the sunken road, with unit after unit falling back under the rain of fire from the Confederate opposition. Finally, they reached a vantage point where they could fire down on the road's defenders. The once seemingly impregnable position had become a death trap. In the last stages of battle, which Union soldiers would later describe as "like shooting animals in a pen," the road rapidly filled with bodies two and three deep. The road soon came to be known as Bloody Lane.

Perhaps the most heroic participants at Bloody Lane were the 69th New York Infantry, part of the famous Irish Brigade. The Union troops attacking the road had been in serious trouble until they caught sight of the emerald banner of the Irish Brigade on the horizon. The Irish announced their arrival with the sounds of drums and volleys of fire as they attacked the Confederate position. As they charged, the brigade screamed loudly and shouted the battle cry *faugh-a-ballaugh* (fah-ah-bah-LAH), Gaelic for "clear the way!"

The thunderous sound of weaponry filled the air as men fell on both sides. The brigade fought fiercely, but battle cries eventually became fainter. The Irish Brigade lost more than sixty percent of their men that day and wrote their name in the bloody pages of American history.

REPLAYING THE PAST?

In the decades since the end of the Civil War, enough strange things have taken place on or around the Antietam battlefield to make many believe that events of the past are still being replayed today. Some who visited have reported hearing phantom gunfire echoing along the sunken road and smelling smoke and gunpowder. Others claim to have seen the apparitions of men in both Confederate and Federal uniforms, often assumed to be reenactors of some event on the battlefield until they abruptly vanish.

Following are four of the places where strange incidents have been reported—three on the battlefield and one in Sharpsburg.

Bloody Lane ✚ Several years ago, a group of boys from the McDonna School in Baltimore took a school trip to Antietam. After touring the battlefield and Bloody Lane, the boys were allowed to wander about and think about what they had learned. They were then asked to record their impressions for a history assignment. The most attention-getting comments were written by several boys who walked down the road to the Observation Tower, located where the Irish Brigade charged the Confederate line.

The boys wrote of hearing strange noises coming from the field near the tower. Some described the noises as a chant, others as a song similar to the Christmas carol "Deck the Halls"—specifically, to the lyrics "fa-la-la-la-la." Had they heard the sounds of the Irish Brigade "clearing the way"?

Another eerie occurrence was reported by battle reenactor Paul Boccadoro of Company G, 96th Pennsylvania Volunteers. One night, after an annual living-history event, Boccadoro and three other men broke off from the dozen or so members who had stopped to rest on the banks of sunken Bloody Lane and walked to the Observation Tower at the end. After a while, the captain sent two men to fetch them, and Boccadoro wrote of what happened next.

"No sooner had those two begun to walk toward us than one of the men who'd stayed on the banks started to hear the sounds of shoes with heelplates—horseshoelike plates we wear on our leather shoes—on the gravel and earth. They first heard two pair of heelplates, then four pair, then six, and so on. They could also hear equipment rustling around on bodies: knapsacks, canteens, and cartridge boxes.

"If anyone knows what it sounds like when men march on a dusty road with full gear on, it's reenactors. Just as the other men began to sit up and peer into the darkness down the road, the sounds faded away as quickly as they came. One man jumped up, went down the road, and looked over the fences and road banks, only to find weeds and small shrubs.

"After talking later that night, we figured that if this was some sort of 'ghost regiment,' it might have followed the two men who had begun to walk down the road to the tower to fetch us." 🖝

A colorized photograph of a portion of Bloody Lane.

☛ "No sooner had those two begun to walk toward us than one of the men who'd stayed on the banks started to hear the sounds of shoes with heelplates—horseshoelike plates we wear on our leather shoes—on the gravel and earth."

A portrait of Lieutenant Colonel James J. Smith [seated in the center] and the surviving officers of the 69th New York Infantry, the Irish Brigade, taken at their camp near Washington, D.C. in May 1865.

A drawing made of the Pry House on the scene by artist A. W. Warren, with a notation on the bottom right, "Gen. Hooker was brought here wounded."

Philip Pry House ✝ This brick farmhouse, which overlooks the battlefield, was commandeered by the Union army's General George McClellan to use as his headquarters during the battle. Shortly after the battle began, General Joseph Hooker was brought to the house for treatment of the wounds he suffered. He was followed by General Israel B. Richardson, who died of painful abdominal wounds at the house more than six months after the battle had ended.

Today the house is owned by the National Park Service and isn't open to visitors—but that hasn't stopped it from spawning strange stories. In 1976, the house caught fire and about a third of it was gutted. It was during the restoration that many unexplained events were recorded.

One day, during a meeting of park personnel, the wife of one of the park rangers met a woman in old-fashioned clothes coming down the staircase. She asked her husband who the lady in the long dress was, but he had no idea what she was talking about.

A short time later, workers arrived at the house to see a woman standing in an upper window—in the room where General Richardson had died. They searched the house, and after going upstairs they realized the room where the woman had been standing had no floor! Could the apparition have been that of Richardson's wife, Frances, who cared for him on his deathbed?

It wouldn't be the last time the ghost was seen. On one occasion, a new contracting crew had to be hired when the original crew working in the house caught a glimpse of the spectral figure and abandoned the project.

It is also reported that phantom footsteps have been heard going up and down the staircase. Might they have belonged to the worried generals, pacing up and down in anticipation of battle? Or perhaps to Fannie Richardson as she climbed the stairs to minister to her dying husband? No one knows for sure, but those who have heard the footsteps are convinced they're not just the sounds of the old house settling. 🐾

General Israel B. Richardson, ca. 1862; Richardson died at the Pry house of his battle wounds and is said to haunt the site.

The Philip Pry house, ca. 1960s; the farmhouse served as Union headquarters during the Battle of Antietam and as a hospital afterward.

Burnside Bridge, an inverted version of a photograph taken in September 1862 by photographer Alexander Gardner.

Burnside Bridge ✠ People who have spent time at the battlefield area known as Burnside Bridge—especially park rangers and Civil War reenactors who have been there after dark—say that strange things happen in the vicinity of the bridge as well. Historians report that the fighting that took place here in 1862 left a number of fallen soldiers behind, and many of them were hastily buried in unknown locations near the bridge. Nighttime visitors to the bridge report seeing blue balls of light moving about in the darkness and the sound of a phantom drum beating out a cadence that gradually fades away.

St. Paul Episcopal Church ✠ Near the center of Sharpsburg is another site connected to the battle: St. Paul Episcopal Church. It was used as a Confederate field hospital following the battle, though it was heavily damaged. Those who have lived close to it claim they've heard the screams of the dying and injured coming from inside the long-since restored church. They have also seen unexplained lights flickering from the church's tower.

The battlefield at Antietam is a place where thousands of soldiers fought, suffered, and perished, their lives ending long before they should have. If ghosts linger because they haven't finished the business of a life cut short, it is hardly surprising that Antietam has more than its share of spirits.

✴ **Antietam National Battlefield Visitor Center, 5831 Dunker Church Rd., Sharpsburg, MD 21782, (301) 432-5124, www.nps.gov/anti/index.htm. Visitor Center is open daily 9 a.m.–5 p.m.; park grounds are open during daylight hours.**

An artist's composite of St. Paul Episcopal Church, in Sharpsburg, which many residents claim is haunted by ghosts of soldiers who died there when it was a field hospital during the war.

THE GREEN ARM OF ANTIETAM

For many years, there was a private museum in Sharpsburg in Washington County, near a pivotal battlefield of the Civil War. The Antietam Battlefield Museum had all the usual relics you'd expect to see at a war museum, but there was one that we bet you've never seen anywhere else: a severed soldier's arm that had dried out and mummified. This creepy body part had clearly not been surgically removed, but blown off its body just below the elbow: Its ragged end was just too messy to be the work of a surgeon—even one who worked a battlefield production line. But the rest of the arm was intact. Shriveled and disgusting, but intact. And it had turned a kind of gross green that made you wonder if it was a sculpture made of copper or bronze. But it was too real-looking to be a fake and just macabre enough to be stuck away in a back room of the museum, out of sight unless you went looking for it.

When the man who ran the museum, John Ray, bought the place back in the 1960s, he apparently had no idea it contained this strange relic. But when he dug it out of the box in the back room where it was filed away, he mounted it and touted it as the Arm of the Unknown Soldier. Now that's the mark of a true museum man—giving a mummified body part a cool name and displaying it proudly.

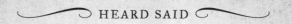
Antietam Days with Dad

I went to the Antietam Battlefield

many times with my dad, who's a Civil War nut. The Battlefield Museum was the high point of our trips. While he was off looking at his stuff, I'd slip into the back room where this creepy exhibit was mounted in its own pine box, and stare at its delicate tapered fingers and well-manicured nails. They say it was the arm of a 19-year-old soldier, but nobody knows whether he was a Confederate or a Union man. When my dad found me looking at this thing one day, I asked him which he thought it was. He looked at me strangely for a while, as if he regretted exposing me to this weird stuff. Then he said, "Look at those fingernails. This was a man who took pride in himself. He's clearly one of ours. Now, let's go get ice cream." So we went. But I'd never have gone if he'd offered to take us out for Slim Jims or beef jerky. ~*Les*

CHAPTER SIX

PENNSYLVANIA

LINCOLN FLAG

The Lincoln Flag is kept in a marvelous building in Milford, PA, called the Columns. This building is also the home of the Pike County Historical Society.

As you walk up the wooden steps and enter through the wide doors, you will feel as if you are stepping back in time. What a magnificent home this must have been. Off to the right, a wide room opens up, and there it is—the Lincoln Flag. This flag was placed under President Lincoln's head after he had been shot. Plainly visible are the bloodstains from the wounded president. Not one of us spoke as we silently examined this most treasured standard.

It seems that after the president was mortally shot by John Wilkes Booth on April 14, 1865, the flag, which had been draped over the balustrade at Ford's Theatre, was placed under his head by Thomas Gourlay, a part-time stage manager at the theater. After the president was moved to the Petersen House, across the street, the flag was taken by Gourlay and eventually was given to his daughter. It was passed down through the family before it was finally given to the Pike County Historical Society in 1954.

Extensive research has confirmed again and again that this is indeed the flag upon which the dying Abraham Lincoln rested his head. It is amazing to see, to almost touch. It is a true American treasure and is right in our own backyard.

— *Dr. Seymour O'Life*

✺ **Pike County Historical Society at the Columns, 608 Broad St., Milford, PA 18337, (570) 296-8126, pikehistorical.org; open Wed., Sat., Sun. 1–4 p.m.**

Previous pages: A reinactment of the Gettysburg battle at East Cemetery Hill in 2013, 150 years after that engagement of July 2, 1863.

An 1865 Currier & Ives print of the assassination of President Abraham Lincoln.

A close-up detail of the bloodstains on the Lincoln Flag, on display at the Columns in Milford.

President Lincoln's box at Ford's
Theatre, Washington, D.C., April 1865.

The barracks at Fort Mifflin, where the ghost of the lamplighter is said to haunt the second-floor balcony.

THE MANY GHOSTS OF FORT MIFFLIN

Theaters of war, it seems, generate more ghosts than any other place. It may be the sheer volume of the dead at the sites of great battles, or the horrors they had endured at the time of their passing. Who knows what the cause may be. But whatever the reason, whenever you find a place where blood had been shed in battle, a ghost story or two cannot be far behind.

Just south of Philadelphia stands a bastion of defense against naval attacks from the Delaware River. The great stone ramparts of Fort Mifflin protected the young nation's capital of Philadelphia against siege ships of the British Empire, which, ironically enough, had partially built the fort in the first place in 1772. But the British destroyed their own defensive handiwork in November 1777 with a pitiless barrage of cannonballs estimated at a thousand rounds every twenty minutes. Nearly three quarters of the defenders perished. The fort

was rebuilt twenty years later and served as a garrison in the War of 1812 and as a prison during the Civil War. It's now a tourist attraction featuring guides in historical dress, but not all of the participants seem to be live actors.

The second-floor balcony of the barracks is said to be visited by the spirit of the lamplighter, the man who lit the oil lamps every evening. Though he's barely discernible in the twilight, people can see he's carrying a long pole with a flickering light on the end.

The casemates are the sites of many other apparitions. The most visible is the Faceless Man, and supposedly, he's the ghost of a war criminal imprisoned in the fort during the Civil War. William Howe was his name, and he was hanged at the fort for the murder of his superior and desertion of duty. When he appears these days, he's fairly easy to see, they say, except that his face is in shadow. The reason? Before hanging, deserters were said to have had their heads covered with black bags as a mark of their shame.

The Screaming Lady is the loudest of the ghosts at Fort Mifflin. She's never seen, but wails from the old officers quarters, where she appears to be living out an eternity of regret for disowning her daughter. She is said to be the soul of Elizabeth Pratt, an eighteenth-century neighbor of the fort whose daughter took up with an officer. Elizabeth renounced and threw out her daughter, who died shortly after from dysentery. The story goes that Elizabeth, consumed with guilt, took her own life. And there is another spectral sound heard at the fort. Near the blacksmith shop, the clash of hammer against anvil often sounds out, only to be silenced when people enter the empty but slightly echoing room.

✸ **Fort Mifflin, 6400 Hog Island Rd., Philadelphia, PA 19153, (215) 685-4167, www.fortmifflin.us; see website for operating hours.**

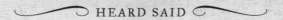
GHOSTLY REENACTOR?

Here is a detail of a photograph taken at Fort Mifflin in 1997 with what appears to be a ghost image. I am a wet-plate photographer doing images on glass using the original process and equipment from the 1860s. This shot was a staged and posed image of the garrison troops of the fort at a Civil War reenactment. I was up on the parapet overlooking the soldiers, and there was no one out there but the troops in formation. At first when I developed the plate, I thought the small markings to the upper-right center were blemishes on the surface of the plate. But looking closer, it appears to be human and not exactly standing on the ground. What is it? I don't know. ~*Ray Morgenweck*

Is the circled "blemish" a ghostly visitor to the reenactment?

GETTYSBURG PHANTOMS

Between July 1 and July 3, 1863, more blood was shed in a formerly little-known Adams County farm community than at any battle in history. The deaths on the battlefield at Gettysburg numbered more than 7,000, and probably a tenth of the wounded died later. With around 10,000 men down in a few horrific days, it's hardly surprising that Gettysburg has its fair share of ghost stories. But oddly enough, one of the stories comes to us from the time of the battle itself.

Although the Confederates were ultimately defeated on July 3, 1863, the Union soldiers were actually in trouble at one point. The 20th Maine Division had arrived to reinforce the flagging troops, but they had no idea where to go. The story goes that a striking figure in an old-fashioned uniform appeared on a white horse and led them to Little Round Top, a strategic point that enabled them to rout a flank of Confederates and ultimately win the battle.

The soldiers insisted that the glowing apparition they followed bore an uncanny resemblance to George Washington. There's no denying this story reeks of propaganda. It is only one step away from the old claim that "God is on our side." But nevertheless, the story has had a remarkably long life.

If you visit the National Military Park on a clear summer night, you will sometimes see fog creeping in and surrounding the field where so many people fell. Fog always brings an eerie sensation with it, and such ground mists are not unusual for this kind of topography. But what's inside the fog is a little more unusual. Lights flash on and off, appearing to advance along the same path that the Confederates had taken to Little Round Top. Sometimes shadows or transparent apparitions appear on horseback. Although it's hard to see anything in those conditions, these riders are often reported as being headless, though this may be due to overactive imaginations fired by too many readings of the Sleepy Hollow legend.

But far and away the most common ghostly phenomena at Gettysburg concern cameras. There were many photographs taken directly after the battle, but it seems nowadays an unusual number of cameras malfunction on the field. Visitors often experience a chill when this happens, maybe because of the weather, maybe from a sudden supernatural fear, or perhaps from the presence of something not of this world.

The view from Little Round Top; on foggy summer nights mysterious lights can sometimes be seen flashing on and off.

A map published soon after the Battle of Gettysburg, entitled *The Union and Rebel Forces in the Cemetery.*

THE GHOSTS OF GETTYSBURG ☞ *Paul J. Forti*

When I was a boy, I remember reading about the Battle of Gettysburg, the most famous battle of the Civil War. During the battle, some 45,000 soldiers on both sides were either killed or wounded. The fighting was intense and terrifying, and many soldiers died of their wounds because of the shortage of medical assistance.

When the battle ended, it left behind a ghastly and ghoulish scene. The smell of death was everywhere, and it was several weeks before all of the dead soldiers were buried. More than 1,200 Confederate soldiers were interred where they fell, in makeshift graves on the main battlefield. The Union soldiers were buried in an extension to the local cemetery, which became the National Cemetery at Gettysburg.

I first visited Gettysburg in May 2000, and I was overwhelmed by the place. I was most impressed with the cemetery. While I didn't believe in ghosts, I had an eerie feeling as I walked over ground holding hundreds of soldiers who died in defense of that in which they believed.

As I finished the tour, I heard about a ghost walk that was provided to visitors, and I decided to take it the next night.

Unfinished graves of dead Confederate soldiers on the field at Gettysburg, photographed by Timothy O'Sullivan.

FROM SKEPTICISM TO BELIEF

The tour started at 8:30 p.m. and was led by a guide dressed in Civil War attire. We visited a number of supposedly haunted sites in the town of Gettysburg and the surrounding battlefields, and it was almost 10:00 when we arrived at the last stop—the National Cemetery.

The tour guide told us there had been many ghost sightings here. He was a good storyteller, and I thought this was part of his act: a way of creating a little excitement for the group. The night was moonless, cool, and quiet. Many people on the tour were asking questions about ghosts, and the tour guide seemed to be embellishing stories he had heard. While I thought he was doing a good job, as a nonbeliever in ghosts I thought much of what he said was mere hype.

So I decided to test the tour guide. I asked him if it was possible to get a photo of an orb on a digital camera. (In the paranormal realm, the word "orb" usually refers to floating, glowing spheres of unexplained origin.) He answered yes, and that he had taken many orb photos with his digital camera.

I decided to try to photograph an orb myself, even though I honestly didn't believe it would happen. I took my digital camera out of its case, turned it on, and tried to find something that I could focus on; it was very difficult to see any headstones or markers. I decided not to use the flash, pointed the camera in the direction of the cemetery, and just hoped for the best.

Not even five seconds had passed before the image appeared on the viewfinder. A woman on the tour was looking at the viewing screen with me, and as the image appeared she screamed, "Oh my God, there's an orb!"

I looked at the screen and saw a series of what looked like small flashlights glowing in the dark. I was thinking, "How could a photo taken in total darkness, where there was no light or reflective material, show any form of light?" Unable to explain it to myself, I turned to the tour guide and asked for his opinion. He looked at the image and said, "Yep, you have a great photo of an orb."

I wasn't convinced that my "orb" photo proved anything, so I returned to the edge of the cemetery alone at 10:00 the next night, where I unsuccessfully tried to reproduce the previous night's results. But as I looked into the distance, I saw an indisputable sight: a soldier dressed in what appeared to be a Union uniform and marching around a group of graves. ☞

I noted that there were no lights or reflections that might cause an optical illusion. I called out to the soldier, but he walked into the darkness. I didn't know what to think.

The next morning I went to the National Park Service headquarters and asked whether any Civil War reenactors had been walking around after dark. A park ranger told me that no one was allowed in the cemetery after dark, nor had there been any rangers on the property at 10:00 the night before. It was at that point that I became convinced that there really are ghosts at Gettysburg.

Over the years, my visits to Gettysburg have made me more of a believer in ghosts. I feel that the more that people believe in the presence of spirits, the greater the chance they will see them. At the same time, I feel that the spirits at Gettysburg are just looking for a little respect. Could it be possible that they present themselves to certain visitors as a way of saying thank you for believing in them?

⊗ **Gettysburg National Military Park:**
Cemetery, 97 Taneytown Rd., Gettysburg PA 17325;
Museum and Vistors' Center, 195 Baltimore Pike (Rte. 97);
(717) 334-1124, www.nps.gov/gett/index.htm. Open 6 a.m.-10 p.m.,
Apr. 1-Oct. 31, and 6 a.m.-7 p.m., Nov. 1-Mar. 31.

Federal casualties at Gettysburg photographed by Timothy O'Sullivan. *Inset*: a modern photograph of Gettysburg National Cemetery by Patricia M. Highsmith, c. 1990.

☞ "As I looked into the distance, I saw an indisputable sight: a soldier dressed in what appeared to be a Union uniform and marching around a group of graves.... I called out to the soldier, but he walked into the darkness."

CHAPTER SEVEN

VIRGINIA
AND
WASHINGTON, D.C.

SPIRITS OF THE SHENANDOAH VALLEY

No period has left a greater mark on the history—and hauntings—of Virginia than the Civil War era. It was a time of great violence, death, and despair for the region. It should come as no surprise to the Weird reader that many of the state's stories of ghosts and phantoms come from this dark time.

It was in the Shenandoah Valley that a man named Colonel John Singleton Mosby, the "Gray Ghost of the Confederacy," commanded the 43rd Battalion of the Virginia Cavalry, or as they were generally known, Mosby's Rangers. The Rangers carried out a successful guerilla war against the Federal forces in Virginia, using hit-and-run tactics to surprise the enemy, derail trains, cut supply lines, and capture literally tons of Union supplies. Though small in number, they soon became one of the most famous legions of Confederate fighters.

Mosby's Rangers fought with honor, something that could not always be said for other guerilla fighters in the Shenandoah, who would pillage and plunder the local populace and indiscriminately kill any Union soldiers who were separated from their units. In retaliation, a group of Federal cavalry soldiers executed seven of Mosby's Rangers, alleging that they had committed atrocities against Union forces in September 1864. Three of the Rangers were hanged and the other four were shot.

Mosby secured permission to execute an equal number of Union prisoners in reprisal. On November 6, he ordered prisoners to draw slips of paper from a hat. The seven men who drew the marked slips were to be killed, just as the seven Rangers had been. After the drawing, the unlucky seven were escorted to the Valley Pike, where they were to be executed as close to Union general Philip Sheridan's headquarters as possible.

But one of the prisoners managed to escape into the forest near Berryville. With Federal patrols in the area, the Rangers decided to go no farther and contented themselves with hanging the six remaining men at a place called Beemer's Woods, north of Berryville. Before the Rangers left, they pinned a note to the clothing of one of the hanged men that explained why they had been executed: "Measure for measure." ☛

Previous pages: A ca. 1900 photograph of the equestrian statue of Robert E. Lee in Richmond, VA, by French sculptor Antonin Mercié. The statue, which stands on Monument Avenue, was dedicated in 1890.

☛ "Local folk who lived near Beemer's Woods often spoke of the eerie sounds and creaking limbs coming from the place where the men had been hanged. Some also claimed to feel a strange presence near the entrance to the woods, as though something remained behind there—something that would never rest in peace."

Colonel John Singleton Mosby, the "Gray Ghost of the Confederacy," stands [clean-shaven] in the center of a group from the 43 Battalion Virginia Cavalry, aka Mosby's Rangers.

Shenandoah Valley, sketched in 1864 by Civil War artist-journalist Alfred R. Waud.

After this event, both sides agreed that neither would harm their prisoners as long as the other side kept to the agreement. Following that, there were no more hangings.

As the years passed, local folk who lived near Beemer's Woods often spoke of the eerie sounds and creaking limbs coming from the place where the men had been hanged. Some also claimed to feel a strange presence near the entrance to the woods, as though something remained behind there—something that would never rest in peace.

It was not the only instance when those executed in the valley returned from the grave. One young man who lived in the Front Royal area was falsely accused by Federal forces of being a member of the Rangers and was beaten to death by a mob of Union soldiers. The ghost of that young man has reportedly returned to the valley many times over a span of years from the 1870s until about 1925. Accounts of his appearances spread fear through entire communities.

One eyewitness, in 1912, was Judge Sanford Johnson, who lived near Riverton. He was outside feeding his dogs one cold winter's day and happened to notice a thin, ragged figure near the creek that crossed his property. He saw the form of a young man in a Confederate uniform and with a cap pulled down low over his brow. The judge said that the figure jerked and stumbled from the creek and then shambled down the long road in front of the house. Johnson did not stay around to see where the ragged figure went next. He ran full speed into the house. He was not sure why he had done so but only knew that the figure filled him with fear. He would later notice that although the figure crossed directly in front of the house, it left not a single track in the freshly fallen snow!

The chilling apparition would appear several more times, but strangely, there have been no reports of him since 1925. Did the wrongly executed young man finally find peace?

THE PHANTOM STAGE

Perhaps the most famous tale of the Shenandoah Valley is the story of the Phantom Stage of Valley Pike. There is little doubt that this tale falls into the realm of ghostly legend, and yet there are some who stubbornly maintain that it is true.

On May 24, 1862, the eve of the Battle of Winchester, General Thomas "Stonewall" Jackson had his army in New Market and was prepared to move against Union general Nathaniel P. Banks, whose troops were gathered nearby. The road that connected New Market to Winchester was a portion of the eighty-mile-long Valley Turnpike. A wide road paved in crushed limestone, it was ahead of its time for nineteenth-century construction, and Jackson used it to great advantage. Moving quickly along the paved road, he was able to fight battles at either end of it within days of each other.

The story of the spectral stagecoach actually begins in New Market. It was said that a Federal spy stole the coach and escaped toward Winchester to warn General Banks of Jackson's impending attack. Shortly after he made off with the coach, two Confederate officers discovered his plans and quickly went in pursuit.

Although the spy had a good lead, the heavy coach hampered his journey, and the Confederate pursuers quickly closed the distance. As they grew closer, lightning flickered across the sky and they could see the man hunched over, snapping the reins and urging the horses to go faster. The Confederates were only yards behind when the spy turned and saw their drawn pistols. He reached into his coat and withdrew his own revolver, then unsteadily tried to aim it at the advancing Confederates as the coach rumbled on. Suddenly, a brilliant flash and a thundering roar swept over the stage and the driver. A bolt of lightning streaked down from the dark clouds above and blasted the stagecoach. It literally exploded into flames, and the driver simply vanished from his seat—utterly destroyed.

The pursuing Confederates were stunned by what they had seen and, after calming their horses, returned to New Market to spread the story. The following day, Stonewall Jackson triumphed at Winchester, thanks to the fact that Banks had no warning of his attack.

Time has passed and the war has long since ended, but they say that on certain nights, when lightning dances across the sky, travelers along the Valley Pike (now U.S. Highway 11) still report seeing a ghostly stagecoach rattling silently along the road. Its driver frantically cracks the reins across the back of the horses, urging them on toward Winchester, still trying to complete his final mission.

The restless spirit of Colonel Charles Blacknall is still thought to haunt the Waverly Farm guest room where he died a far from peaceful death in the wake of a major Confederate defeat.

Opposite: An 1890 lithograph depicting the Battle of Cedar Creek, October 19, 1864, the decisive battle in the Shenandoah Campaign that became a turning point for the Union victory.

THE GRAY MAN OF WAVERLY FARM

By the fall of 1864, the Shenandoah Valley had become the most hotly contested piece of ground in Virginia. It was vital to the Confederacy for its location and for the rich stores of food and crops that could be found there. For this same reason, the Federals were intent on destroying it. That season became known as "the time of the burning." During this period, one of the great ghost stories of the Civil War took root at a place called Waverly Farm.

It was there that Colonel Charles C. Blacknall, commander of the 23rd North Carolina, had been taken after being wounded in the foot on September 19, 1864. At the time, Blacknall and his men had been fighting alongside the Berryville Pike, about three miles east of the town of Winchester. The Union soldiers were advancing, beating back the Confederates, and the colonel was deeply worried about the fate of his men.

At Waverly Farm, the colonel's condition worsened, except briefly on October 17 when he heard cannon fire in the distance, from the Battle of Cedar Creek. He asked his servant to help him into his uniform, and he hobbled over to the window, hoping to be reunited with his troops. But the guns grew distant, and Blacknall realized that the Confederates had lost. Heartbroken, he returned to his bed—and never rose from it again. Even the amputation of his leg at the knee did not stop the spread of infection, and he died at Waverly on November 6. Blacknall was buried in nearby Stonewall Cemetery beside his fallen comrades from the 23rd North Carolina, but the legends say that he does not rest here in peace.

The sightings of the "Gray Man" at Waverly began a short time after the war. The first reports came when a woman named Mrs. Joliffe was visiting the family who owned the farm. She was asleep in the guest room—the same room in which Blacknall died—when the opening of the door awakened her. She was surprised to see a man in a gray Confederate uniform walk across the

room and stop at the window. It seemed as though the man was watching for someone.

Mrs. Joliffe was not accustomed to having strange men appear in her room at night, and she demanded to know what the man was doing there. He gave no answer and in fact seemed oblivious to anyone else's being there. After several minutes, he bowed his head as if disappointed and turned away from the window. Then he was gone. The description that she would later provide matched that of Colonel Blacknall, right down to the shape of his face and the color of his hair.

She was not the last to see the depressed colonel take up his post in the guest bedroom. In fact, sightings continue to today. Those who have encountered the apparition report the same things. They tell of the sounds of footsteps entering the room and the ghostly figure, watching and waiting. Sometimes a figure is seen from outside, framed in the room's window. All the reports are of a man in a gray uniform who matches the description of Colonel Charles Blacknall.

Why does his ghost remain here at Waverly? Or does he remain at all? Could the energy of Colonel Blacknall's dying days and his disappointment over the Confederate loss have left a mere impression on the place, one that keeps repeating itself over and over again? Perhaps . . . or maybe Blacknall's spirit has simply never found rest. Perhaps he is still waiting for the return of the Confederate army—a day that will never come.

VIRGINIA BATTLEFIELD GHOST

The terrible ten-month siege of Petersburg from June 1864 to April 1865 apparently left a host of spirits behind at Fort Stedman, a Union stronghold during the Civil War. The siege was a grueling affair that trapped the Confederate army and left it starving inside the city. On March 25, 1865, the Confederates launched a desperate attack on Fort Stedman. Much to the surprise of both sides, the Southern forces took the fort quite easily. They then turned their attention to nearby Fort Haskell, where the attack fell apart as the Confederate troops began gorging themselves on captured Federal supplies. Four hours after the fighting began, they broke off the attack, just a few weeks before Lee's final surrender at Appomattox Court House.

Despite the fact that the Union actually carried the day at Petersburg, it is said that the ghosts of Federal troops remain behind here. According

An 1865 stereograph of Fort Stedman, where apparitions and ghostly music have been seen and heard.

to a reliable witness who was at Fort Stedman early one summer morning, he noticed a group of Union soldiers on a ridge. They were formed up in a battle line facing the fort. The witness was more than a little surprised to see them, as he knew of no reenactments that had been scheduled to take place there. He stood watching them for several minutes—and then they abruptly disappeared.

A former park supervisor also reported hearing the sounds of music coming from a ridge where a Union corps was encamped during the siege. He swore the music was popular patriotic songs from the Civil War period like the "Battle Hymn of the Republic" and "The Star-Spangled Banner." Although he tried, he was never able to find an explanation for the eerie, and possibly spectral, music.

✹ **Fort Stedman site is part of the Petersburg National Battlefield, which has numerous locations in Petersburg; www.nps.gov/pete/index.htm.**

LINGERING GHOSTS OF KALORAMA

The Kalorama estate once occupied a large site in northwest Washington, D.C., land that is now the 2300 block of S Street NW. The house had its share of tragedy over the years, but it was not until the Civil War that its walls became a shelter for death and horror—terrifying elements that linger to this day.

General John Bomford purchased the estate in 1812. Bomford was a close friend of naval hero Stephen Decatur and his wife, Susan. Bomford even allowed Commodore Decatur's body to be buried in a tomb on the estate after he was killed in a duel. But it seems Decatur did not rest happily there. It is said that blood from his wound would sometimes appear on the outside of the tomb and that this is why his wife finally had the body removed to Philadelphia, where his parents were buried. The removal stopped the bloody stains from appearing on the stone walls of the crypt. During the Civil War, many of the larger homes in the District of Columbia, including Kalorama, became hospitals for soldiers wounded in nearby battles.

Hundreds of soldiers were treated and cared for in the mansion and on the grounds of the estate, and some of its ghostly tales come from this time.

When the war ended, in April 1865, many soldiers were still recovering from their wounds and were unable to return home to their families. They lingered at Kalorama for months, and on Christmas Eve decided to throw a party. Unfortunately, a defective stovepipe caused a fire to break out, which spread through the entire east wing of the house before it was brought under control. Several soldiers died; the building was badly damaged, but most of it was saved.

Within months, tales started to be told about the ruins of the mansion's east wing and about the "sinister shadows" that were seen there and on the grounds of the estate. It was said that screams and moans could be heard, coming from the darkness. The reports became more prominent as the years passed. Area residents who braved the early evening darkness to strollamong the remains of the estate said they encountered "moving" or "roaming" cold spots. Some of them were described as being accompanied by unexplained odors that seemed to be the smells of blood, morphine, sweat, and gunpowder.

Eventually the growing population of Washington took over Kalorama, and what was left of the house was replaced with a newer home in the early 1900s (several decades later that house was flattened when the street was widened). There are those who say that even though the estate has vanished, the cold spots and the sickly smells still remain. And that a few former patients of the Kalorama hospital still linger behind.

Opposite, near right: The ruins of Kalorama Hospital in Washington, D.C., photographed after the Christmas Eve fire of 1865.

Far right: General John A. Logan, photographed by Mathew Brady, ca. 1864.

> "Tales started to be told about the ruins of the mansion's east wing and about the 'sinister shadows' that were seen there and on the grounds of the estate. It was said that screams and moans could be heard, coming from the darkness."

LOGAN'S STILL LOOKING FOR HIS HORSE

General John Alexander Logan, or "Black Jack" Logan as he was affectionately called by his men during the Civil War, was elected to the U.S. Senate in 1871. As a staunch Republican and chairman of the Military Affairs Committee, he used his strong influence to develop Reconstruction policies.

Several years after installing air-conditioning ducts in the basement of the Capitol, workmen discovered a room that had been sealed off. Inside the room was a stuffed horse that bore a strong resemblance to the horse that Logan sits astride in the famous Logan Circle statue. It was discovered that when the horse died, the general had it mounted and displayed for a time in the Capitol building to remind everyone of his battlefield exploits during the war. Since the discovery, staff workers have claimed that General Logan's ghost roams the basement corridors, still looking for his favorite horse.

THE GHOST OF HONEST ABE

There is no doubt that few presidents left the sort of mark on the White House that Abraham Lincoln did. When he was assassinated, his plans for reconciliation between the North and South were interrupted and his work was left incomplete. In fact, some would say that it remains incomplete, even today. Perhaps this is why his spirit is so often reported at the White House and may explain why he is our nation's most famous ghost.

In the years following Lincoln's death, staff members and residents often reported mysterious footsteps in the hallways. One of the earliest reliable reports from someone who actually saw Lincoln's apparition came from President Theodore Roosevelt, who took up residence in the house nearly forty years after Lincoln's death. "I see him in different rooms and in the halls," the president admitted. In truth, it comes as no surprise that Roosevelt may have "attracted" the ethereal presence of Lincoln, as he greatly admired the former leader and quoted his speeches and writings often.

President Calvin Coolidge's wife, Grace, encountered Lincoln, who she said was dressed "in black, with a stole draped over his shoulders to ward off the drafts and chills of Washington's night air." She also saw him on another occasion in the Yellow Oval Room, which had been Lincoln's library during his tenure in the White House. Poet and Lincoln biographer Carl Sandburg stated that he felt Lincoln's presence close to him in the Yellow Oval Room.

During World War II, Queen Wilhelmina of the Netherlands spent the night in the White House. She was sleeping in the Rose Room when an insistent tapping on the door awakened her. Assuming the summons must be important, she quickly opened the door, only to see Abraham Lincoln standing there. The queen passed out, awakening on the floor later. The ghost had vanished.

During his time in office, President Dwight D. Eisenhower made no effort to deny the experiences that he'd had with Lincoln's ghost. He told his press secretary, James Haggerty, that he frequently sensed Lincoln's ghost in the White House. One day, he explained that he was walking down a hallway when he realized the figure approaching him from the opposite direction was Abraham Lincoln. Eisenhower took the encounter in stride—after the horrors of war, the specter of Lincoln was probably a welcome sight.

☛ "One day, [President Eisenhower] . . . was walking down a hallway when he realized the figure approaching him from the opposite direction was Abraham Lincoln."

Despite official denials, members of the First Families continued to encounter Lincoln's specter. When Gerald Ford was in office, his daughter, Susan, publicly acknowledged her belief in ghosts and made it clear that she would never sleep in the Lincoln Bedroom—or "that room," as she called it. According to one account, Susan actually witnessed Lincoln's spirit.

There were no reports of Lincoln's ghost during the elder Bush's administration, and none by the younger Bush either (other ghosts were reportedly seen by George W. Bush and his daughter Jenna). However, during the Clinton years, there were at least two sightings. President Clinton's brother Roger admitted one encounter. In the second instance, a Clinton aide said that he had seen Lincoln walking down a hallway. The story, which was briefly reported in the news, was quickly denied and dismissed by the White House as a joke. As of this writing, no reports of Lincoln's ghost have filtered out of the White House concerning the current president, Barack Obama, although First Lady Michelle Obama reported being awakened by strange sounds from the hallway outside the presidential bedchambers. Who knows what stories will be told in the years to come?

Does the ghost of Abraham Lincoln really walk in the White House? Some of our country's most influential leaders have certainly believed so. But why does he still walk here? Is the apparition merely a faded memory of another time or an actual presence? Or does the ghost appear, as has been suggested, during times of crisis, when perhaps the assistance of the president who faced America's greatest crisis is most needed?

✳ **The White House, 1600 Pennsylvania Ave. NW, Washington, D.C. 20500. To schedule a tour of the White House, visit www.whitehouse.gov/about/ tours-and-events for more information.**

One of the last photographs of President Lincoln, this ghostly portrait, was taken by Henry F. Warren on the White House balcony, March 6, 1865.

The Lincoln Bedroom at the White House, photographed by Jack E. Boucher, ca. 1960s.

THE HAUNTINGS OF JEFFERSON DAVIS

Perhaps two of the most tragic figures connected to the Civil War era were the men chosen to lead the opposing sides in the conflict, U.S. president Abraham Lincoln and Confederate president Jefferson Davis. Both suffered terribly during the war, torn apart over what the country was enduring. Each man also suffered great personal losses during these years of strife, and not surprisingly, both are said to walk among us today as ghosts. In Davis's case, two very different locations in Virginia are associated with hauntings, each connected to tragedies suffered by him during and after the Civil War.

The first location is the home that served as the "White House of the Confederacy," located on Clay Street in Richmond (now part of the Museum of the Confederacy). There is every indication that the Davis family was happy here, despite the pressures of the war and the agonizing hours that President Davis spent working, often until the darkest hours of the night. Davis's only comfort after the long hours of work was his family. He often said that they eased his mind for precious minutes every day, especially his children, whom he constantly indulged.

Davis's special favorite was little Joe, who had just turned five in April 1864. He often remarked that Joe was the hope and greatest joy in his life. Unfortunately, Joe Davis was taken away all too soon. On April 30, 1864, he was climbing on the railing of a balcony in back of the house when he lost his balance and fell to the brick pavement below. The fall fractured his skull, and he died a short time later. Over the next days, cards and letters flooded the Davis home, including a heartfelt message from Abraham Lincoln, returning the gesture that Davis had made to Lincoln when his son Willie had died. Joe was buried in Hollywood Cemetery in Richmond. Shortly after, Davis had

Jefferson Davis [seated center], and his wife Varina [far right], ca. 1885, pose for a portrait at their home in Beauvoir, MS, with their daughter Margaret, three grandchildren, and servants.

The "White House of the Confederacy" on Clay Street in Richmond, photographed in 1865.

the balcony that his son fell from removed from the house and destroyed.

When Federal forces took Richmond on Sunday, April 2, 1865, Davis and his family escaped. At least, his living family escaped.

The same might not be said for little Joe Davis. After the family left Richmond, dozens of witnesses reported seeing the apparition of a little boy who resembled Joe wandering aimlessly near the Confederate White House. The boy was oblivious to passersby and was heard to walk back and forth, muttering, "He's gone! He's gone!" just before vanishing in front of startled witnesses. Would Joe be forever trapped in search of his father?

The Davis family had more immediate concerns. It was during their time of flight that Abraham Lincoln was assassinated, and most believed that Jefferson Davis had somehow been involved. In May 1865, a contingent of Federal cavalry found Davis and quickly arrested him, though he denied being involved in the assassination plot.

Davis and his wife were transported by ship to the country's most escape-proof prison of the day, Fort Monroe. While there, Davis was imprisoned in a cell that was barely better than a dungeon. He was kept in solitary confinement for four months, his arms and legs bound in chains, until public sentiment forced his captors to remove them and place him in better quarters. Davis was released on May 13, 1867, after two years of confinement.

Though Jefferson Davis did not die in Fort Monroe, numerous witnesses have reported sighting apparitions in and around the cell at Fort Monroe where he was imprisoned. Most of the sightings have been of strange mists and energy masses of different shapes and forms, but most witnesses believe the ghost seen here is that of

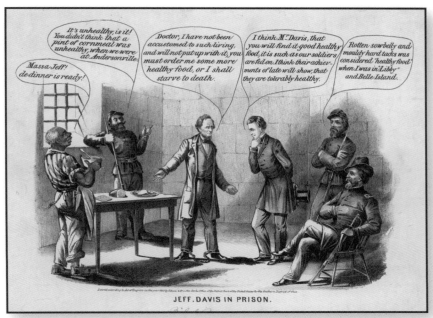

A satirical political cartoon of Jefferson Davis in prison, 1865.

Davis, perhaps reliving the ordeal that he suffered. Mrs. Davis is also said to appear on late evenings and has been spotted in the second-floor window of quarters directly across from where her husband was held.

After Davis died in 1889, his body was moved from two different cemeteries before Confederate veterans convinced his wife to bury him in Richmond's Hollywood Cemetery, in 1893 (see pages 140–41). Davis's final burial there resolved the family's other ghostly story. The body of little Joe Davis was also moved and placed beside his father, finally reuniting them. Strangely enough, after being seen in the vicinity of the Confederate White House for over thirty years, the apparition of the little boy who cried, "He's gone!" was never seen again after that.

✪ **Museum of the Confederacy, 1201 E. Clay St., Richmond, VA 23219, (804) 649-1861, www.moc.org; open daily 10 a.m.–5 p.m.**

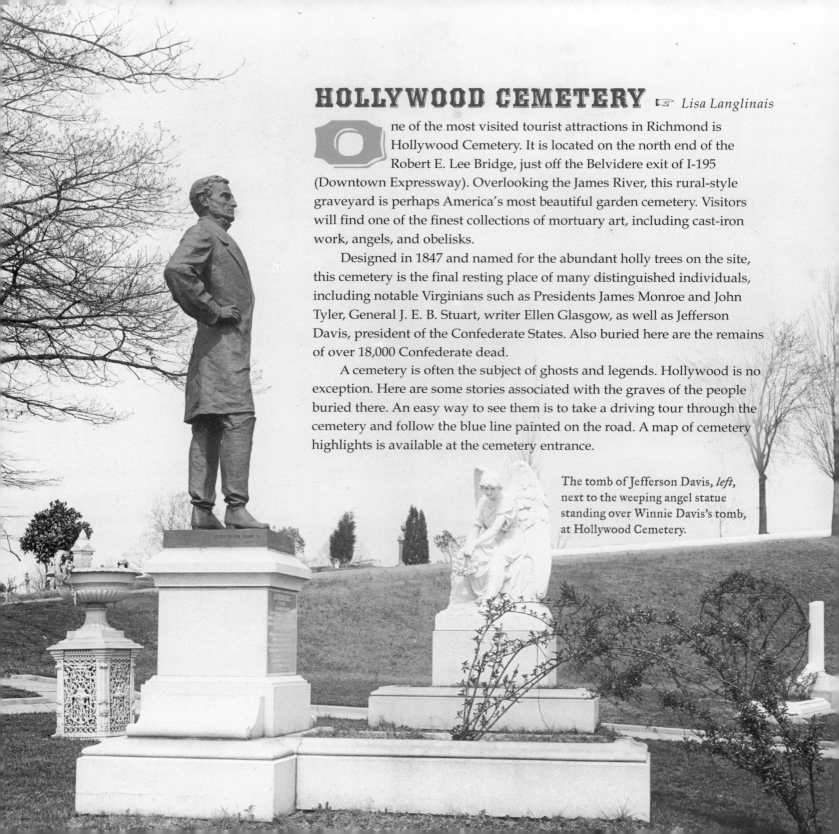

HOLLYWOOD CEMETERY ☞ *Lisa Langlinais*

One of the most visited tourist attractions in Richmond is Hollywood Cemetery. It is located on the north end of the Robert E. Lee Bridge, just off the Belvidere exit of I-195 (Downtown Expressway). Overlooking the James River, this rural-style graveyard is perhaps America's most beautiful garden cemetery. Visitors will find one of the finest collections of mortuary art, including cast-iron work, angels, and obelisks.

Designed in 1847 and named for the abundant holly trees on the site, this cemetery is the final resting place of many distinguished individuals, including notable Virginians such as Presidents James Monroe and John Tyler, General J. E. B. Stuart, writer Ellen Glasgow, as well as Jefferson Davis, president of the Confederate States. Also buried here are the remains of over 18,000 Confederate dead.

A cemetery is often the subject of ghosts and legends. Hollywood is no exception. Here are some stories associated with the graves of the people buried there. An easy way to see them is to take a driving tour through the cemetery and follow the blue line painted on the road. A map of cemetery highlights is available at the cemetery entrance.

The tomb of Jefferson Davis, *left*, next to the weeping angel statue standing over Winnie Davis's tomb, at Hollywood Cemetery.

WEEPING WINNIE DAVIS

After first being buried in New Orleans, Jefferson Davis was moved to Hollywood Cemetery in 1893. Here he rests with his other family members, including his daughter Winnie. Winnie is said to have died from a broken heart because she unfortunately fell in love with a Yankee. Her young beau, Alfred Wilkinson, was the grandson of a staunch abolitionist and was rejected by Jefferson Davis when he asked for permission to marry Winnie. Winnie's health began to deteriorate over the next year, so much so that her father changed his mind. But he changed it too late. Winnie died at the age of thirty-four without ever marrying. An angel in mourning stands at her grave and is said to shed real tears.

CONFEDERATE PYRAMID

In the Confederate section of the cemetery stands a ninety-foot pyramid made of rough-hewn Richmond granite. It was completed in 1869, and no mortar was used in its construction. The pyramid is a monument to the 18,000 Confederates buried here, including Davis, Stuart, George Pickett, Matthew Fontaine Maury, and the first Confederate soldier killed during the war, Henry Lawson Wyatt. Twenty-three Confederate generals are buried here, as well as soldiers from battles around Richmond. The Confederate dead exhumed from Gettysburg in the 1870s were reinterred here on what is now known as Gettysburg Hill. In the cornerstone are entombed various Confederate artifacts, including a flag, a button from Stonewall Jackson's coat, and a lock of Jefferson Davis's hair.

When visiting near the pyramid, many people have reported seeing orbs, feeling "cold spots," sensing their energy drain, and becoming ill the next day.

Hollywood Cemetery, 412 S. Cherry St., Richmond, VA 23220, (804) 648-8501, www.hollywoodcemetery.org; open daily 8 a.m–5 p.m.

The pyramid at Hollywood Cemetery honoring the 18,000 Confederates buried there, photographed by Carol M. Highsmith.

The Tombstone House of Petersburg.

TOMBSTONE HOUSE

If any residence holds the potential for mass haunting, the Tombstone House in Petersburg is surely it. Such fearful probabilities simply have to accompany a home constructed of some 2,200 marble tombstones, particularly since these markers were pulled off existing graves. All the headstones used in its 1934 construction were "harvested" from the nearby Poplar Grove National Cemetery. Even more noteworthy is the fact that each one of them came from the grave of a Union soldier who had died at the siege of Petersburg during the Civil War. This last bit adds a devilish touch of retribution to an already bizarre tale.

So how did it happen? Why, simple economics, of course!

It seems that during the Depression era, maintenance costs were strangling the Poplar Grove Cemetery. Petersburg National Battlefield Park superintendent Benjamin F. Moore determined that money could be saved on maintenance if all upright grave markers were cut and laid flush with the ground. Under his orders, the markers were pulled from each individual plot, their bottom portions trimmed off, and the upper portions, replete with inscriptions, positioned flat on the ground, faceup. Since the stones were made of valuable marble, the lower portions were retained for later sale.

This brings us to one Oswald E. Young, who quickly snapped up these lower portions for the anything but princely sum of forty-five dollars. His intent? Why, to build his very own two-story Tombstone House, of course!

This he did, and the rest is pretty much standard history, at least insofar as anything regarding a tombstone house can be seen as standard. As testament to the relative normality involved here, there has been no reported haunting of this house despite the strong implications, and any out-of-the-ordinary bad luck has not befallen anyone. Yet.

But the Tombstone House is not without controversy. There are those who maintain that the markers used in the home's construction were in fact the upper portions that contained the inscriptions—not the lower ones. In this scenario, the written words are said to face inward and wall plaster relegates them to anonymity, for now. Then there are others who say that such a thing would never have been done; it would have been far too ghoulish.

Since there is no reliable list of Union dead buried in Poplar Grove during the period of the siege, this question will likely remain with us until Tombstone House reaches its own day of reckoning, and a heavy swinging ball offers up final answers to the mystery.

Today, anyone who walks up the Tombstone House's tombstone path (yes, this too is made out of grave markers) can readily sense the dark playfulness of this morbid idea come to, er, life. And in fact, the home is still in use as a residence, rented out by its current owner.

✴ **The Tombstone House is a private residence and is not accessible to the general public.**

STRONG [BURIED] ARM OF THE CONFEDERACY

Talk about tragic ironies. Thomas "Stonewall" Jackson, the legendary Confederate general known for his role in such Civil War skirmishes as Second Manassas and the Battle of Antietam, was, in the end, removed from this earth not by a Union army bent on revenge but by his very own troops. History shows this certainly wasn't born of ill will, but rather was a case of mistaken identity. However, it is not this substantial footnote to history that warrants the general's inclusion in this chapter. It is what happened to Jackson's left arm, after the fact, that we find most curious.

The unthinkable occurred on May 2, 1863, during the battle of Chancellorsville. On that fateful night, after a fruitful assault that netted the Confederate general the capture of Union troops, Jackson decided to scout out his defeated enemy, hoping to cut off their line of retreat. He headed out with a small group of soldiers. Later, as they made their way through the dark woods back to their own lines, one of the men in the Confederate North Carolina regiment saw the returning general's horse. Fearing it was the Union cavalry attacking, the man shouted, "Halt, who goes there?" Not giving Jackson's group sufficient time to reply, he fired a shot at the approaching figure. Startled by the sudden gunfire, other Confederates fired blindly into the darkness.

Three musket balls tore into Jackson's left arm during the confusing barrage, destroying ☞

General Thomas "Stonewall" Jackson, photographed ca. 1863.

arteries and fracturing the bone below the shoulder. The wounded general was placed on a stretcher and carried by his men to a field hospital set up in a nearby drinking establishment called the Wilderness Tavern.

To find out more about the incident, we spoke with Frank O'Reilly, one of the historians at the Fredericksburg and Spotsylvania National Military Park.

Weird Civil War: Frank, doesn't a tavern seem to be an odd choice of place to bring the wounded general?

Frank O'Reilly: Well, you know it was an excellent choice of a hospital at that time. They had various things that they could take care of the patients with. There was a nice creek that ran through here, which was a great water source for the different hospitals. Amputations were a tremendously grisly process. What they would do is simply take a knife and cut a semicircle around the spot where the wound occurred and pull back the skin to expose what's left of the bone. At that point, they would saw across the bone and then tie off the arteries, bring the flap around, and also suture that up.

WCW: And what was the usual practice with the amputated limbs? Did they just discard them?

FO: Normally, all the limbs would have been placed in a pile and immediately after the battle would calm down, they would have buried them in a mass pit.

WCW: So who had the foresight to go rescue this limb from the pile so it wasn't buried in a mass grave with all the others?

☛ "The general's final words were, 'Let us cross over the river and rest in the shade of the trees.'"

FO: The person who rescued Jackson's arm was actually Jackson's chaplain, a man named Beverly Tucker Lacy. He had just joined Jackson a couple of months before and was completely fascinated by the general. He was the right man in the right place at the right time, because he showed up in the field hospital right after they amputated the arm. If he had been there ten minutes later, he wouldn't have even seen the arm.

What Reverend Lacy actually did was take it back to the surgeon who amputated the arm, and asked him to identify it. Dr. Hunter McGuire was absolutely certain it was Jackson's arm; he had just removed it a couple of minutes before. At that point, Reverend Lacy wrapped up the arm, took it across the fields to his home, Ellwood, and buried it in the family cemetery. Burying the arm was just a way to pay homage to their general. Stonewall Jackson was literally the most famous person in North America at this particular time.

The following day, Jackson was moved to a nearby plantation. Just when it looked as if he might survive his dire skirmish, pneumonia set in. He succumbed six days later, on May 10. The general's final words were, "Let us cross over the river and rest in the shade of the trees."

The Jackson arm still rests on the grounds of Lacy's humble family plantation, Ellwood, under a stone that proclaims: **"ARM OF STONEWALL JACKSON, MAY 3, 1863."**

The resting place of Stonewall Jackson's arm on the grounds of the Ellwood Manor at the Fredricksburg & Spotsylvania National Military Park.

Frank took us to pay our respects at the small burial ground, located in the middle of a cornfield.

FO: We are in an area that would have had nothing but field hospitals all around us, and Jackson's chaplain walked up this hill on May 4 and buried the arm right here. After the war, another one of Stonewall Jackson's staff officers, a man named James Power Smith, actually put this monument out here so we wouldn't forget this spot.

WCW: Didn't somebody try and dig it up once?

FO: Actually, it's been dug up a couple of times. As it turns out, Union soldiers dug up the arm during another battle, in 1864, but reportedly reburied it right away. The arm apparently rested in peace again until 1921, when a marine corps general named Smedley Butler came across the gravestone while on maneuvers in the area with his men.

Butler was quite a maverick. He thought that it was something of a Southern myth, so on a whim he decided to debunk the myth and ordered the grave dug up. There's at least one account that alleges that he had a group of marines dig up this spot, figuring that they would get a big open hole and a laugh at the locals, but what they unearthed was actually an arm that had been amputated.

WV: So what did they do with it?

FO: Well, the story goes that they reburied the arm with full military honors.

✪ **Fredricksburg & Spotsylvania National Military Park**, (540) 654-5121, www.nps.gov/frsp/index.htm; see website for different addresses and hours for numerous sites in the park, including Chancellorsville Battlefield and the Ellwood Manor.

HIS BOOTS WERE MADE FOR WALKING ☞ *Paul J. Forti, Ph.D.*

The Battle of Ball's Bluff occurred on October 21, 1861, in Leesburg, VA, and it was one of the first Civil War battles that tested the strength of the Confederacy. They did well, sending the Union Army running scared back across the Potomac. During the battle, Union colonel Erasmus Burt of Mississippi was seriously wounded. That evening, he was taken to an upstairs bedroom in Harrison Hall, a house located about a mile from the battle. Burt died the following day, and several years after the war rumors about his ghost roaming Harrison Hall were heard throughout the community.

Those stories continued into the current century, although ownership of the house changed several times. Once a private residence, it became a bed-and-breakfast, business conference center, a career-management consulting firm, and then changed its name to the Glenfiddich House in the early 1990s.

An illustration from the *Illustrated London News* of November 23, 1861, captioned "the retreat of the Federalists after the fight at Ball's Bluff."

For a period, the owner lived in the top floor of the home with his wife, whom I'll call Ms. Smith. The first time I stayed there, in the spring of 2006, she told me about her experiences with the colonel. During the late 1990s, back problems forced her to remain in bed for several months in the room where Colonel Burt had died. She swore she heard and saw the colonel on several occasions.

I didn't hear or see anything unusual during my stay. The owners gave me a tour of the home and told me its original owners were distant relatives of General Robert E. Lee. Lee visited several times during the war, and in 1862 he planned the battle of Antietam in the dining room with his staff, including Stonewall Jackson.

The history intrigued me, but I remained skeptical about the colonel's ghost, even after hearing that other visitors saw him walking down the hall in his leather boots, rattling his sword. My feelings changed in August 2006, when the owners invited me to stay at the Glenfiddich House again.

This time, I had Colonel Burt's old room. After getting into bed at 11 p.m., I awoke two hours later to a strange sound down the hall. I attributed the noise first to heating pipes (before remembering it was summertime) and then to air-conditioning (it was a cool evening, and there was no need for it). I became concerned—I was the only person in the house and had no idea where the sound was coming from. I listened closely but didn't hear anything else, so I relaxed and began to fall back asleep. Fifteen minutes later, I heard what sounded like footsteps coming down the hallway. As they got closer, I could hear the dull clang of metal as it rubbed against leather bootstraps. It sounded like the steps of a person wearing riding boots.

At first I was too scared to get out of bed, but I forced myself to do so, turning on the lights in my room. The sound promptly stopped. I grabbed a flashlight, opened the bedroom door, and walked around upstairs, but saw nothing. Back in the room, I left the light on and got back into bed. Ten minutes later, I again heard heavy boot-clad footsteps walking down the hall. I called out, "Who is there?"and the sound stopped. Once again, I got out of bed, opened the door, and shouted out, "Who is there?" but heard nothing.

I climbed back in bed and fell asleep, only to awaken to footsteps at about 4 a.m. I went through the same drill as before, but this time I stood at the door and shouted: "Go away, whoever you are!" It must have had an impact, because now I could make out the faint figure of a man walking down the steps to the first floor. I immediately turned on every light and went downstairs, finding nothing.

A few hours later I got dressed and went downstairs, where Ms. Smith had arrived with breakfast. When I brought up my overnight experiences, she said, "I guess you finally met the colonel." She told me he usually appears after he is comfortable with a guest, and though mischievous, he is not harmful. After her encounters with the colonel, he no longer bothered her.

I was alarmed and excited by what had happened, but I managed to finish my business in the area that day and headed home. A few weeks later, I received a certificate from the owners saying that I survived a night with the colonel.

I don't know where Colonel Burt is buried, but I can tell you where he's waiting for his next guest. As for me, I don't plan on being anywhere his boots will be walking again. Should I return to the area, I will stay someplace that has no ghostly claim.

⊛ **The Glenfiddich House is home to a private business and is not accessible to the general public.**

CHAPTER EIGHT

THE MIDWEST

ILLINOIS, INDIANA, MISSOURI, OHIO & WISCONSIN

Republican campaign banner, 1860. The printer changed Lincoln's name to "Abram" to fit the design.

Abraham Lincoln, congressman-elect from Illinois, photographed by Nicholas H. Shepherd in Springfield, 1846.

Previous pages: President-elect Abraham Lincoln on the porch of his home in Springfield, IL, with his sons Willie and Tad, in February 1861.

THE DARK PROPHECIES OF ABRAHAM

No book about the unusual characters and eccentric figures of the Civil War would be complete without an in-depth portrait of Abraham Lincoln, favorite son of Illinois. The death of his mother when he was still a child, hard labor to make an existence for himself in the wilderness, and his struggle for an education all combined to make him a serious man. While he always stated that he longed for a life of peace and contentment, he seemed to know that he would never live to find it. It's not surprising that legend has it that Lincoln's ghost is one of the most restless in American history (also see pages 136–37).

Many people who knew Lincoln during his Illinois years described him as seeming to be in a world by himself, ignoring his surroundings and, at times, even visitors to his law office. He would sit for several minutes in complete silence, staring straight ahead. A few friends described him as rejoining the visitors "like one awakened from sleep" when such an interval ended. Years later, in Washington, a number of distinguished foreign visitors noted this strange habit. One French nobleman counted "twenty such alterations" in a single evening.

One of his closest friends and longtime law partner, William H. Herndon, stated that Lincoln was "a peculiar, mysterious man . . . [he] had a double consciousness, a double life. The two states, never in the normal man, coexist in equal and vigorous activities though they succeed each other quickly."

Lincoln was elected to the presidency in 1860, and while he may have won the day, he fared poorly in the popular vote. He had soundly defeated Stephen Douglas in the electoral college but had won just forty percent of the vote among the people. When Lincoln returned home in the early-morning hours after the votes had been counted and he knew he had won, he went into his bedroom for some much-needed rest and collapsed onto a settee. Near the couch was a large bureau with a mirror on it, and Lincoln stared for a moment at his reflection in the glass. He then experienced what many would term a vision, one that he would later believe had prophetic meaning.

In the mirror, he saw that his face appeared to have two separate, yet distinct, images. The tip of one nose was about three inches away from the other one. The vision vanished but appeared again a few moments later. Lincoln realized that one of the faces was actually much paler than the ☞

☞ "Lincoln was 'a peculiar, mysterious man . . . [he] had a double consciousness, a double life.'"

☛ **"There is no doubt that the most crippling blow he suffered in the White House was the death of his son Willie, in 1862."**

other, almost with the coloring of death. The vision disappeared again, and Lincoln dismissed the whole thing to the excitement of the hour and his lack of sleep. But he talked of the strange experience for many years to come.

As the Civil War raged, its bitter turmoil and the great loss of life took their toll on Lincoln. He became bitter and dark, his times of prayer and contemplation grew much longer, and he seemed to turn inward. He spoke often of the "hand of God" in certain battles, and it was almost as if an uncanny perception somehow strengthened as the war raged on. Documents of the Union war department refer to one occasion when Lincoln burst into the telegraph office of the department late one night. He ordered the operator to get a line through to the Union commanders. He was convinced that Confederate soldiers were just about to cut through the Union lines.

The telegraph operator asked where he had obtained such information, and Lincoln reportedly answered, "My God, man! I saw it."

While the war affected President Lincoln deeply, there is no doubt that the most crippling blow he suffered in the White House was the death of his son Willie, in 1862. Lincoln and his wife, Mary, grieved deeply over the twelve-year-old boy's death.

It was probably the most intense personal crisis in Lincoln's life.

After his son died, Lincoln tried to work, but his spirit had been crushed. One week after the funeral, he closed himself up in his office and wept all day. Some said he was on the verge of suicide, and he withdrew even further into himself.

He also began to look more closely at spiritual matters.

While Lincoln never publicly discussed having interest in spiritualists, Mary embraced them openly and invited a number of them to the White House. Each claimed to be able to allow Mary to communicate with Willie. Mary's closest spiritualist companion was Nettie Colburn Maynard. Many are familiar with a tale told about a séance held by Maynard in 1863 where a grand piano levitated. The medium was playing the instrument when it began to rise off the floor. Lincoln and Colonel Simon Kase were both present, and it is said that both men climbed onto the piano, only to have it jump and shake so hard that they had to climb down. Lincoln would later refer to the levitation as proof of an "invisible power."

Perhaps the most famous weird incident connected to Lincoln would be his prophetic dream of his assassination.

WILLIE LINCOLN, THIRD SON OF PRESIDENT LINCOLN.
DIED FEBRUARY 20, 1862, AT THE AGE OF 12.
From a photograph taken by Brady at Washington, shortly
before the death of Willie Lincoln.

William "Willie" Lincoln,
photographed by Mathew Brady in 1861.

One of Lincoln's old friends from Illinois was a lawyer named Ward Hill Lamon, whom Lincoln appointed to a security position in the White House. Lamon would never forgive himself for Lincoln's assassination—especially since he believed that he had had a forewarning of the event from the president himself. For just shortly before Lincoln was killed, he had recounted to Lamon and Mary an eerie dream of death. Lamon recorded Lincoln's recitation of the dream in his book *Recollections of Abraham Lincoln* (1895):

About ten days ago, I retired very late. . . . I soon began to dream. There seemed to be a death-like stillness about me. Then I heard subdued sobs, as if a number of people were weeping. I thought I left my bed and wandered downstairs. There the silence was broken by the same pitiful sobbing, but the mourners were invisible. I went from room to room; no living person was in sight, but the same mournful sounds of distress met me as I passed along.

It was light in all the rooms; every object was familiar to me; but where were all the people who were grieving as if their hearts would break? I was puzzled and alarmed. What could be the meaning of all this? Determined to find the cause of a state of things so mysterious and so shocking, I kept on until I arrived at the East Room, which I entered. There I met with a sickening surprise. Before me was a catafalque, on which rested a corpse wrapped in funeral vestments. Around it were stationed soldiers who were acting as guards; and there was a throng of people, some gazing mournfully upon the corpse, whose face was covered, others weeping pitifully.

"Who is dead in the White House?" I demanded of one of the soldiers.

"The President," was his answer, "He was killed by an assassin!"

Then came a loud burst of grief from the crowd, which awoke me from my dream. I slept no more that night; and although it was only a dream, I have been strangely annoyed by it ever since. ☛

Lincoln spoke of death and prophecies to other members of his staff also, like Colonel William H. Crook, one of his bodyguards. On the afternoon of April 14, Lincoln told him about the strange dreams that he had been having. Crook pleaded with the president not to go to the theater that night, but Lincoln dismissed his concerns, explaining that he had promised Mary they would go. Lincoln had a habit of bidding Crook a good night each evening as he left the office. On that fateful day, according to Crook, Lincoln paused as he left for the theater and turned to the bodyguard. "Good-bye, Crook," he said significantly.

"It was the first time that he neglected to say good night to me," Crook would later recall. "And it was the only time that he ever said good-bye. I thought of it at that moment, and a few hours later, when the news flashed over Washington that he had been shot, his last words were so burned into my being that they can never be forgotten."

This ghostly sketch by artist William Waud of President Lincoln's catafalque on view at the State House in Springfield, IL, seems to be a tragic fulfillment of Lincoln's dream.

The ghostly remains of
what was Hop Hollow Road.

BODIES IN THE WOODS ALONG HOP HOLLOW ROAD

Illinois' first penitentiary was opened in Alton in 1833. Conditions were bad right from the beginning, and the prison became known as a grim and horrific place, plagued by rats, vermin, and disease. The health of the prisoners was completely broken while they were incarcerated, and many of the men died within months of their release.

By the 1850s, conditions were so bad that Dorothea Dix, a social reformer, began a crusade to close the Alton prison. Her complaints brought about a legislative investigation that eventually led to the construction of a new prison near Joliet. In May 1859, Alton prisoners began to be transferred to Joliet, and the Alton penitentiary was finally abandoned in 1860.

Abandoned for civilian prisoners, that is. Soon the prison was fixed up enough to pass military inspection, and it reopened in 1862 as a military facility to hold Confederate prisoners.

Within three days of the arrival of the first Confederate soldiers, the penitentiary was already overcrowded. While the maximum capacity of the institution was eight hundred, throughout most of the war it held ☛

☛ "Throughout most of the war [Alton penitentiary] held between one thousand and fifteen hundred prisoners. . . . [It] was plagued by lice, rats, countless diseases."

between one thousand and fifteen hundred prisoners and often more. Just as it was in former times, the prison was plagued by lice, rats, and countless diseases, including a smallpox epidemic that claimed a great many lives.

When a prisoner died, soldiers observed the same procedure as the penitentiary guards had followed. The men on burial detail loaded the body onto a raft and floated it up the Missouri to a ferry landing not far from the prison. The body was then placed in the back of a wagon and transported along a wooded trail known as Hop Hollow Road. The path wound through the forest, around the bluffs, and through Hop Hollow itself. Eventually, it ended in an area in North Alton that had been turned into a cemetery by the original prison officials. The body was placed in a shallow grave, and a numbered stake was placed over it. An undertaker recorded what information existed about the man, and he became the next line in the ledger book—until another prisoner died and the process was repeated all over again.

Or at least that was supposed to be how it worked. Stories have long circulated that the soldiers attached to burial detail would never actually make the entire trip up Hop Hollow Road to the burial ground. Rather, they would stop the wagon along the roadway somewhere and dump the corpses in the woods. A bottle would be broken out, and the soldiers would play cards and drink for the amount of time it would have taken to transport and bury the bodies.

I admit that I was skeptical when I first heard this story, but one thing I've learned over the years is that at the heart of every legend lies a kernel of truth, no matter how small. Hop Hollow Road is no exception.

One day, about six months after hearing this story for the first time, I spoke with an Alton police officer who had once answered a call about a body found near what was once Hop Hollow Road. Today, the largest part of this road no longer exists. A faint trail leading away from the highway is all that can be found. It curves into a heavily wooded area (which is private property) and comes to an end at Holland Street. Beyond it, the remains of the road become Rozier Street, which passes by the Confederate Cemetery. This police officer was told that a body had been discovered in the woods near the crossing of Holland and Rozier. When he arrived, he found a collection of old bones that, apparently, had been there since sometime around the Civil War. Could this have been the remains of one of the Confederate prisoners?

As it happened, bodies being left in the woods was not the only fantastic portion of the story about the duty-shirking Union soldiers. In fact, it was only the beginning.

The legend went on to say that the ghosts of these improperly buried Confederates refused to rest in peace and that they returned to haunt Hop Hollow Road. Over the years, their apparitions had been seen along the roadway. As time passed, the tale was expanded to include the fact that these ghosts not only walked the road near where their bodies had been left but that they also signaled passing vehicles in hopes of getting a ride! A ride to where? To the cemetery where their bodies were supposed to have been laid to rest, of course. Those luckless drivers who did pick up one of these passengers were always shocked when the hitchhiker simply vanished without a trace from the seat beside them. At that point, so the story goes, they realized that they had picked up a ghost.

Could such a story be true? I'll leave that up to you, but if you do happen to be driving along the street off Hop Hollow Road some night and you see someone near the edge of the woods, waving his arms and looking for a ride . . . drive on.

Chains of the Dead Still Heard on Hop Hollow Road

I don't go out looking for the unusual.

If anything, I've always been a skeptic. In fact, I still am, despite what happened to me one night many years ago along a road in Alton. Did I encounter something supernatural? Some may say yes, others no. I myself am still not sure.

This incident occurred about ten years ago. I was working the midnight shift at a convenience store near Alton. I'd often be the only one on the road as I made my way home early in the morning. I was driving a 1982 Monte Carlo that was falling apart at the seams. Many nights I found myself cursing as I made makeshift repairs to the car alone on some roadside.

This was one of those nights. I had gotten a flat tire and pulled off next to a patch of woods. It was no big deal at all really; by this point, I had become a master at changing flats—it wouldn't take me more than ten minutes. Those ten minutes, though, gave me a story that I still tell today.

I began to hear a sound emanating from the woods as I worked with the tire. "Chink . . . chink . . . chink . . ." It was methodical, and sounded like chains banging together. They freaked me out. They got progressively louder and closer to me. I have never worked faster at changing a tire than I did that night. I wrapped up, threw my tools into the trunk, and got in the car. Just as I did, I heard a low moaning noise accompanying the clanking of the chains, which now seemed to be just at the edge of the tree line. I got out of there fast. I've never been more scared in my life.

I tried to think of a rational explanation for the noises, but couldn't come up with any. I did some research and found out that those woods lie along what was once known as Hop Hollow, an area where many Confederate soldiers had their bodies dumped after they died in a nearby prison. Many friends have told me that the only explanation for what I heard was that a ghost, bound in chains, was approaching me for help.

Despite my experience, I would say that I still generally don't believe in ghosts. However, when it comes to Hop Hollow, I'll never travel that road again without AAA! *~Andy D.*

GREENWOOD CEMETERY ☞ *Troy Taylor*

Exactly when people were first interred at what is now Greenwood Cemetery in Decatur, IL, remains a mystery. First used as a burial ground for native peoples, it began to be used as a graveyard by settlers sometime in the 1820s. It also may be the site of the graves of runaway slaves. In 1857, the cemetery was officially incorporated into the city of Decatur, and by 1900 it had become the place to be buried. But its prominence was short-lived and in 1920 the cemetery went bankrupt. The grounds soon became overgrown and the graves fell into disrepair.

It was the desolation of the cemetery's oldest part that led to the stories and legends that would haunt the place for years to come. When the city of Decatur took charge of Greenwood in 1957, it also took responsibility for maintaining the cemetery. Still, the graveyard's reputation stuck. Stories of ghosts and the unexplained mingle fact with fiction and are told to this day.

PRISONERS OF WAR

One of the graveyard's best-known ghostly denizens is the Prohibition-era Greenwood Bride, but if visitors to the site are to be believed, she has company: soldiers who were buried in a mass grave on a desolate hill in the far southwest corner of Greenwood Cemetery.

During the Civil War, Decatur was on a direct line of the Illinois Central Railroad, which ran deep into the South. The line continued north and connected to a railroad that went to Chicago. Here, it reached Camp Douglas, a prison for Confederate soldiers. Many trains came north carrying Union troops bound for Decatur and beyond. Soldiers aboard these trains were often wounded, sick, and dying. Occasionally, deceased soldiers were taken from the trains and buried in Greenwood Cemetery, which was very close to the train tracks.

In 1863, a prison train holding more than a hundred rebel prisoners pulled into Decatur. Many of them had contracted yellow fever in the diseased swamps of the South. The Union officers in charge of the train had tried to separate soldiers who had died in transit, but to no avail. Many of the men were close to death, and it was hard to tell who was alive and who wasn't.

The bodies were removed from the train and taken to Greenwood Cemetery, where they were unloaded and stacked at the base of a hill in the southwest corner—possibly the least desirable spot in the cemetery. The hill was so steep that many of the gravediggers had trouble keeping their balance. In a portent of what was to come, perhaps, it was the last place anyone would want to be buried. The men hastily dug shallow graves and tossed the bodies of the Confederates inside. It has been said that without a doctor present, no one could have known if all of those buried were actually dead. Some may have been inadvertently buried alive—no doubt the reason why this is said to be the most haunted section of Greenwood.

Decades of reports tell of ghosts and strange energy lingering about the hill. Visitors, many of them knowing nothing of the hill's bizarre history, have seen mysterious lights and heard voices, footsteps in the grass, whispers, and cries of torment. Some even claim to have been touched or pushed by unseen hands. There are also reports of soldiers returning from the other side of the grave, with visitors seeing what they described as transparent men in uniform walking among the tombstones. Could the Confederate soldiers who were buried so haphazardly on the hill be determined to make themselves known to the living?

✸ **Greenwood Cemetery, 606 S. Church St., Decatur, IL 62522**

☞ "Decades of reports tell of ghosts
and strange energy lingering about the hill.
Visitors, many of them knowing nothing of the hill's bizarre history,
have seen mysterious lights and heard voices,
footsteps in the grass, whispers, and cries of torment."

Five Confederate prisoners of war at
Camp Douglas Prison, Chicago, IL, ca. 1863.

WOLF MAN OF VERSAILLES

Warren Zevon made us all familiar with piña colada–drinking werewolves in his song "Werewolves of London." But only from Indiana comes the strange tale of an ex–Civil War soldier who officially joined a wolf pack and became something like a wolf himself.

As the story goes, a man known as Silas Shimmerhorn was fighting for the Confederates as part of John Morgan's Raiders. As the band of men neared Versailles in 1863, they were intent on disrupting the Union forces' supply route. But something happened along the way, and for some reason Shimmerhorn broke ranks from the rest of the Raiders and hid out in the woods of Versailles. This would seem to be a simple case of desertion, but then things got weird. The legend says that he wandered through the woods for a while before finally settling into what has become known as the Bat Cave—a cavelike structure that is now part of Versailles State Park. In the beginning, we can assume that Shimmerhorn used his gun to get food. But it was only a matter of time before his ammunition ran out. Plus there was the fact that the Union forces, and now the Confederates, would be searching for him, so any gunshots might attract attention. Consequently, Shimmerhorn took to hiding out in the cave during the day and then creeping out under the cover of darkness to raid local farms.

Shimmerhorn also had another, more pressing, problem: the pack of wolves that had moved into the area and were intent on claiming the Bat Cave for their own. We're not sure what type of negotiation skills Shimmerhorn had, but they were obviously pretty darn good, because he and the wolves apparently struck up a deal to join forces and live in the cave together. What's more, legend says that Shimmerhorn became part of the pack and started running and hunting with them. Perhaps that's the reason that local farmers would often come across animal carcasses bearing marks from the teeth of wolves, along with some strange markings and puncture wounds they were unable to identify.

As time went on, locals began seeing a naked man with long, scraggly hair and a beard running in their fields at night alongside a pack of wolves. As more and more cattle were killed, the farmers decided to band together and track down these animals, as well as the person that they were now calling the Wolf Man of Versailles.

Vintage engraving of a wolf pack attacking sheep; did Silas Shimmerhorn join the Versailles wolf pack on their hunting forays?

One story claims that a farmer spotted the pack entering the Bat Cave and ran to tell his neighbors. When all of them were armed, they proceeded to the entrance of the cave, where they were met with the most ferocious snarling they had ever encountered. Their lamps were not bright enough to pierce the darkness of the inner cave, so they had no idea what they were walking into, but the snarling they heard made them aware that, guns or no guns, they were incredibly outnumbered. At that point, the farmers chose to retreat from the cave's entrance.

But they hadn't given up completely. They decided to not enter the cave again while the pack was so large. But every time the pack was spotted running through fields, farmers would open fire. No one ever managed to get a clear shot at the Wolf Man, though. Or maybe it was simply because he still looked too much like a man for someone to be able to take aim and fire at him.

The farmers had no problem shooting the wolves, though, and soon the pack's numbers began to dwindle until they were all but gone. It was then that a few brave souls decided it was time to try to reenter the Bat Cave. This time, there were no growls and snarls coming from the entrance. As the men made their way to the back of the cave, they found it empty except for an old straw bed and a rifle with "SS" engraved on it. That would seem to be the end of this weird story, but it's not, for even today there are reports that the area around the Bat Cave resounds with the howls of wolves late at night. Sometimes people catch a glimpse of a ghostly pack running through the woods. And running along with them is the spectral form of an unkempt man with long hair and a beard.

A portrait of the intrepid couple who served together in the Union army: John and Elizabeth Finnern; from *History of Decatur County, Indiana: Its People, Industries and Institutions,* by Lewis Albert Harding, 1915. The inscription on their gravestone in Greensburg reads: "She Served in Male Attire Until Her Sex Was Detected When she was Detailed as a Nurse Serving 3 Years."

SOLDIER WOMAN

Residents in and around Greensburg, IN, often came to the home of Civil War veteran John Finnern to listen to stories of battle—but it was not John they came to hear. The recollections and adventures so many wanted to relive were the war stories told by his wife, Elizabeth!

Elizabeth Cain Finnern could tell the most exciting stories because during the war she posed as a Union soldier and fought for more than six months before her masquerade was discovered. Even after it was learned that the gallant soldier was actually a woman, Elizabeth remained with the fighting unit, leaving only to nurse her wounded husband and other sick and injured men.

What led her to carry out this elaborate ruse and risk her life on the bloody battlefields of the Civil War?

John and Elizabeth Finnern came to America from Germany in the 1850s and not long after found their adopted country embroiled in a civil war. Anxious to protect the freedoms he had recently acquired, John enlisted in the Union army in 1861. He planned to leave Elizabeth behind on their Ohio farm, but she refused to stay alone; instead, she volunteered as a nurse-laundress for the military.

There are different stories as to how Elizabeth ended up as a soldier on the field of battle. Some say that she simply donned a Federal uniform she found in a storeroom and joined her husband on the battlefield.

She spent the next several months disguised as a man, never leaving John's side. She lived as a soldier, carrying a rifle, enduring long marches, going without food, and taking part in several battles. She also cared for the wounded and helped with amputations, leading many to believe that other soldiers may have been aware of her secret.

The Finnerns fought side by side at the battles of Corinth, Pocahontas, and Huntsville, AL; Harrison, MO; and Pulaski, Fort Donaldson, and Chattanooga, TN, among others. When John was wounded at the Battle of Arkansas Post, Elizabeth reportedly charged the Confederate lines and gunned down the man who had wounded him. Another Ohio soldier who had followed after her managed to save Elizabeth from death or capture.

It was at this point that her real identity was revealed, but she didn't let this stop her from caring for her husband—and saving hundreds of other lives. Following John to the hospital, Elizabeth was stunned to find that he was among more than seven hundred wounded men. The unit was disorganized and had no director, so she took over the supervision of the doctors, nurses, and scarce medical supplies. Not only was she credited with renovating the hospital, but she successfully battled an outbreak of scarlet fever as well.

When John was mustered out of the service in September 1864, the couple moved to Indiana. In the years that followed, they enjoyed great fame there as a result of their wartime exploits. After John's death in 1905, Elizabeth became a recluse. Few people visited her, and the town of Greensburg largely forgot about her. One winter she became desperately ill; luckily, one of her few remaining visitors was a female doctor whom she had inspired as a child years before. She nursed Elizabeth back to health and then helped her to apply to President Theodore Roosevelt for a pension as a soldier's widow.

Elizabeth died in July 1907, the pension funds largely unspent. Since Elizabeth had no family to pass the funds on to, her doctor friend put it to fitting use: a Bedford stone monument to mark the graves of two battlefield soldiers named John and Elizabeth Finnern.

✳ **South Park Cemetery, 405 S. East St., Greensburg, IN 47240, (812) 663-4468; the Finnern grave site is located in Soldiers' Circle.**

☛ "When John was wounded at the Battle of Arkansas Post, Elizabeth reportedly charged the Confederate lines and gunned down the man who had wounded him."

1859 JAIL AT INDEPENDENCE ☞ *James Strait*

In 1981, Mike Gillespie was a college student who worked as a docent in the 1859 Jail Museum in Independence, MO. It was a low-key job that let Mike guide visitors through the museum—which counted outlaw Frank James (older brother of Jesse) and Confederate guerrilla William Quantrill among its infamous inmates—and still have time to do schoolwork. Mike had worked at the museum for only a few weeks when he heard footsteps on the upstairs floorboards. Thinking visitors may have slipped in without his noticing, he left the front office and climbed the stairs, finding only the portrait of Benoni Hudspeth hanging on the wall. Hudspeth was an Independence resident who left for the California Gold Rush in 1849 and was subsequently murdered. The portrait's painted eyes had a creepy habit of following people as they walked up the steps.

Mike initially attributed the footsteps to creaking floorboards, but he soon began to note a pattern of unexplainable phenomena. An alarm system would go off after having been correctly set, requiring him to re-enter the building and walk the dark hallway past the original six jail cells. He hated this, because he always felt compelled to look into one specific jail cell.

Museum visitors regularly commented that the building left them with an uneasy feeling. One afternoon, Mike fell into a conversation with a psychic who had just completed a twenty-minute tour of the jail. The psychic, visibly shaken by his brief experience in the museum, explained that he had sensed much malevolence and death in the building. The pair then embarked on a room-by-room tour of the facility, beginning upstairs. Mike described the footsteps he'd heard, and the psychic explained that the original marshal's wife had been pregnant and that the pacing in the upstairs room was that of the expectant father. As the two started downstairs, the psychic noticed Hudspeth's portrait and reached out to touch it. He was immediately repelled. . . . Hudspeth's spirit [the psychic said] was a permanent resident in the building.

They moved on to the downstairs rear portion of the jail. The psychic was drawn to one unit in particular—the same cell that Mike repeatedly felt compelled to look into when walking past. Although deeply unsettled by the energy emanating from the cell, the psychic extended his arm through the slatted iron door. The hair on his forearm immediately rose. According to the psychic, someone had been killed in the cell and the angry presence wanted out. The vengeful spirit didn't want anybody else in there, either.

The psychic moved on to the marshal's office and remarked that the room had an overwhelming sense of death. Mike knew that the marshal had indeed been killed in that office, and he was impressed when the psychic pointed to a spot, saying the deceased had fallen there.

Museum records indicate that a man by the name of Jim Knowles had been incarcerated at the 1859 Jail during the Civil War for his connection with the Union militia, which had been harassing or stealing from the families of Confederate soldiers. When the Confederates took possession of the jail during the battle at Independence, they administered their own form of justice by shooting Knowles in his cell. Which one he occupied isn't known.

POPPING REALITY

Signs of an incarcerated spirit emerged again when a high school student visited the museum one afternoon. She and Mike struck up a conversation while standing in the jail's gift shop, and when she asked Mike if the jail housed any ghosts, he said, "Naw." At that moment, an inflated balloon on display in the shop popped. The student insisted that Mike had popped it to scare her, but he maintained his innocence.

Later that day Mike inflated a balloon and said, "Okay, if there is a ghost in here, let's see you break this balloon." The balloon popped. Mike chuckled over the coincidence, picked up another balloon, and announced, "Okay, I don't believe this. If the ghost of Jim Knowles or William Quantrill or Frank James is here, let's see you break this balloon." This time as Mike was tying off the end of the balloon, it popped in his hand.

In 1982, Mike turned his responsibilities over to a college student with whom he shared his ghostly encounters. The new docent soon got in touch with a local radio station and arranged for a Halloween séance with an experienced psychic. A twelve-year-old female cousin of the new docent, who happened to be sensitive, stood off to the side of the table during the séance and, at one point, ran hysterically into another room. As it turned out, she had looked into the same jail cell that had caused the first psychic's arm hair to stand on end and spotted a man wearing a long dark coat with metal buttons. So who was the phantasm? Jim Knowles is the most likely candidate, and although it isn't known which unit he occupied, the cell where Mike, the psychic, and the young cousin all sensed a ghostly presence is an obvious possibility.

If you're a ghost hunter, thrill seeker, or die-hard skeptic, the 1859 Jail may be the venue to reinforce the connection between our material world and the world of footsteps, vaporous shadows, and mysterious energies. Go prepared with a handful of balloons and some bare forearms, as they may be your most useful investigative tools.

✸ **The 1859 Jail, Marshal's Home and Museum, 217 N. Main St., Independence, MO 64050, jchs.org/1859-old-jail. Open Apr. 1–Oct. 31, Mon.–Sat., 10 a.m.–4 p.m.; Sun., 1–4 p.m.**

The haunted cell block in the 1859 Jail.

The final, unmarked resting place of Eliza Haycroft at the Bellefontaine Cemetery in St. Louis.

UNMARKED MADAM

A lonely grave site sits overlooking Cypress Lake, in the Bellefontaine Cemetery in St. Louis, MO. It contains the remains of a person who performed a valued, if somewhat notorious, service for the country during the Civil War.

Eliza Haycroft was a well-known madam in St. Louis. She and her ensemble of ladies of the night satisfied the needs of countless Civil War soldiers and other clientele in the city. Her services were a matter of common knowledge and her business was allowed to exist in relative peace. The people making the decisions that allowed it to exist—and to thrive—were, of course, powerful persons of the male sex, even perhaps clients.

However, in typical hypocritical style, when Madam Haycroft died, there was much angst about how she should or could be buried.

Bellefontaine Cemetery was her choice, but the self-righteous of that time did not want her buried in what was then a new and prestigious burial ground. Ultimately, they allowed her to be buried on a very pretty hillside in the cemetery, but there was a caveat. For her to rest in Bellefontaine, she had to lie without a grave marker.

So it was then, and so it is today. Eliza Haycroft forever sleeps, unmarked, in Block 20, Lot 2076.

✹ **Bellefontaine Cemetery, 4947 W. Florissant Ave., St. Louis, MO 63115, (314) 381-0750, bellefontainecemetery.org**

ZOMBIE ROAD ☞ *Troy Taylor*

Traveling west along what used to be old Route 66, you soon leave the buildings and houses in the western suburbs of St. Louis behind as you enter a rugged, wild Missouri landscape of forests, rivers, and caves. It is here that mysteries lie.

If the stories told about one forgotten stretch of roadway are even partially true, then a place called Zombie Road may be one of the weirdest spots in the region. Zombie Road (a name by which it was known at least as far back as the 1950s) was once listed on maps as Lawler Ford Road. (Where the "Lawler" came from is lost to time, but a ford crossed the river here.) People were sometimes ferried across the river at this location, which no doubt explains why the road was placed here.

The road may have originally been an American Indian trail that was later converted into a roadway by European settlers. The railroad came through the area in 1853, and in 1868 the Glencoe Marble Company started to quarry the nearby limestone deposits in what is now the Rockwoods Reservation. A side track was laid from the deposits to the town of Glencoe, and Lawler Ford Road became a gravel and dirt road providing access to the railroad tracks and the Meramec River. It's likely that wagons were used to haul quarry stone up the road, and trucks later were used on the narrow road, which was paved at some point.

TALES TAKE SHAPE

The quarry operations were shut down and the road fell into disuse. Those who recall the road during that period say that the narrow, winding lane, which runs through roughly two miles of dense woods, was always enveloped in a strange silence and a half-light. Shadows were long, even on the brightest days, and it was impossible to see past the trees and brush to what was coming around the next curve. If you were driving and met another car, one car would have to back up to one of the few wide places on the road to allow the other car to pass.

Thanks to its seclusion and abandonment, in the 1950s, Lawler Ford Road became known as a lovers' lane and a party spot for local teenagers. It still sees a traveler or two today, though most who come here are hardly looking for a party. Instead, they come for a taste of the unexplained.

Like many similar locations, Lawler Ford Road gained a reputation for being haunted. Numerous legends and stories exist, from the typical tales of murdered boyfriends and killers with hooks for hands to more specific tales of a local killer who was dubbed the Zombie. Supposedly living in a dilapidated shack by the river, he was said to attack young lovers who wanted someplace quiet and out of the way. As time passed, the stories of the madman were told and retold so often that the road's original name was largely forgotten, replaced by Zombie Road — the name it is known by today.

Even now, there is no shortage of stories about the road. Resident ghosts include a man killed by a train in the 1970s and a mysterious old woman who yells at passersby from a house at the end of the road. The tales of American Indian spirits and modern-day devil worshippers could fill a small book.

Is there any truth to the ghost stories — or at least a history that could explain how they got started? For the answer, read on.

American Indian Spirits ✢ There is no record of the first inhabitants of the area, but they were probably the Indians who built the centuries-old Cahokia Mounds, located near present-day St. Louis. Many other tribes passed through the region as they were moved out ☛

A *Harper's Weekly* illustration of Union army volunteers being attacked by a mob of Confederate sympathizers in St. Louis, MO, June 1861—an example of the violence that perhaps might explain some of the strange occurrences along Zombie Road.

of their original lands in the east, but they never stayed. If these indigenous people left an impression behind, it could be the reason why Indian spirits are still encountered here today.

Civil War Soldiers ✛ During the Civil War, the city of St. Louis found itself in the predicament of being loyal to the Union in a state predominantly dedicated to the Confederate cause. For this reason, men in the Home Guard were picketed along the roads and trails leading into the city. Confederate spies, saboteurs, and agents used less-trafficked paths to get in and out of the area, including the trail that would later be known as Lawler Ford Road. Troops from the Home Guard were stationed at the ford, and a number of men died here in short battles with them.

Could this violence explain some of the hauntings along Zombie Road? It's possible that the bloodshed that occurred here during the Civil War left its mark on the site, as it has on so many other locales.

The Railroads ✛ The railroads figure large in stories of the road. Della Hamilton McCullough, the wife of a local tanner and shoemaker, was killed in 1876 after being struck down by a railroad car. It may be her death that started the Zombie Road legend of the ghost of the person who was run over by a train, since there's no record of fatal train accidents in modern times.

Today, the old line can still be seen at the end of the road, where it is believed the railroad ghost walks. Many accounts over the years have described a translucent figure in white who walks up the abandoned line. Those who've claimed to see it say the phantom glows with bluish-white light but always disappears if anyone tries to approach it.

Some of the other restless ghosts could be those of accident victims along the rail line. Sharp bends in the tracks at Glencoe were the site of frequent derailments—so many that eventually service was discontinued around the bend in the river.

Many of the people I've talked with about the strange happenings on and around Zombie Road speak of unsettling feelings and the sensation of being watched. Some felt they were being followed on the trail, as though someone was trying to keep pace with them, although they saw no one. Also, it's not uncommon for visitors to report seeing the shapes or shadows of presences in the woods, some of which have been mistaken for actual people until the hiker confronts them and finds no one there. . . .

I have to confess that when I first began researching the hauntings of Zombie Road, I thought they were little more than myths that arose from the vivid imaginations of generations of teenagers. I never expected to discover the dark history of violence and death in the region or anything that might substantiate the tales of ghosts and supernatural occurrences. It was easy to find people who believed in the legends of Zombie Road, but I never expected to be one of those who came to be convinced.

✵ **Zombie Road is now part of the Rock Hollow Trail in Wildwood, MO (the main trailhead is located at 777 Ridge Rd.); www.cityofwildwood. com/390/Rock-Hollow-Trail.**

NO RETREAT FOR CONFEDERATE SOLDIER

In 1861, federal authorities authorized the construction of a Confederate prisoner of war camp in northern Ohio. Lieutenant Colonel William Hoffman, the U.S. commissary-general of prisoners, visited the Sandusky area and began looking for a location for the prison, focusing his attention on the Lake Erie islands. After rejecting several of the islands because of their proximity to Canada and/or their high civilian population, Hoffman settled on the unpopulated Johnson's Island.

Using lumber from trees on the island, a stockade covering approximately sixteen acres was built, complete with a fifteen-foot-high fence surrounding it. Inside were thirteen two-story prisoner barracks and a hospital. Construction was completed within the year, and in 1862 the first prisoners arrived from Camp Chase in Columbus. Over the course of the next four years, over eleven thousand Confederate officers and enlisted men would come to be imprisoned on Johnson's Island.

By all accounts, life at the island prison was better than average most of the year. However, the frozen winds that blew across Lake Erie made for brutal winters, especially since the vast majority of Confederate prisoners were used to warmer climates. It didn't help matters when the green lumber used to construct the prison shrank over time, causing holes and gaps to appear in the prison walls. Inmates tried to fill the holes with newspaper, but this did little to hold back the cold. Add to all of this the fact that the limestone in the soil made for poor drainage, causing the privies to overflow with waste, and you are left with some rather horrific living conditions.

After the prison closed down, the island was essentially abandoned. However, in the 1890s, the area enjoyed a brief revival of sorts when the Johnson's Island Pleasure Resort opened up. But when Cedar Point Amusement Park moved in nearby, the resort quickly began losing money and soon fell into ruin. Eventually, Cedar Point purchased the resort and razed or moved all of the remaining buildings.

Today, while visitors to the island can see an earthen fort, all that remains of the Civil War prison is the cemetery, which houses more than two hundred graves. The centerpiece is a large bronze statue of a Confederate soldier. This statue faces north as opposed to south, which would have symbolized a retreat. However, legends abound of the statue's coming to life at night and moving.

In addition to the moving statue, there are reports of the ghosts of Confederate soldiers, which have been seen walking among the tombstones and under the trees surrounding the cemetery. A few people even claim to have heard the disembodied voices of the imprisoned men.

There is also a strange legend involving

Above: An 1865 map of Johnson's Island showing fortifications, the prison [on the right side of the map in the enclosed space], and other buildings; *inset*, a recent photograph of the Confederate cemetery on the island.

a group of Italian immigrants hired to work at the nearby quarry. It is said that although many of the workers did not speak English, for some unknown reason they began singing "Dixie."

A taunt to the unfortunate Confederates? If so, as far as we know, none of the singing immigrants earned a place in the graveyard.

✳ **Johnson's Island Museum and Information Center, Ohio Veterans Home, I.F. Mack Bldg., 3416 Columbus Ave., Sandusky, OH 44870, www.johnsonsisland.org. Open weekends and holidays from Memorial Day to Oct. 1, 1 p.m.–4 p.m. (Johnson's Island is a private residential area accessible by causeway. The only area open to the public is the Confederate cemetery.)**

Opposite: The bronze statue of a Confederate soldier on the monument in the cemetery on Johnson's Island; it was dedicated in 1910 by the United Daughters of the Confederacy.

THE LADY IN GRAY ☞ *Andrew Henderson*

A melancholy ghost haunts the rows at Camp Chase Confederate Cemetery, on the west side of Columbus, OH. Known as the Lady in Gray, she usually weeps quietly over the grave of one Benjamin F. Allen, a private in the 50th Tennessee Regiment, Company D. Allen's grave is number 233 out of 2,260 Confederate soldiers laid to rest in this two-acre plot in the capital city of a very Northern state.

The cemetery in Columbus's Hilltop neighborhood marks the place where a prisoner of war camp stood more than 140 years ago, though at the time the location was well outside the city limits. In May 1861, a Union military training ground named Camp Jackson was established here. By July of that year, when the first prisoners were admitted, its name was changed to honor President Lincoln's Secretary of State (and later Chief Justice of the United States), Hamilton County native Salmon P. Chase.

At first, Camp Chase took only officers as prisoners; enlisted men were imprisoned at Fort Warren, near Boston Harbor. A large number of the officers were captured during 1862 Union victories at Fort Donelson, TN, and Mississippi Island No. 10. But by the beginning of 1863, some eight thousand men of every rank were incarcerated behind the high-staked walls of the camp, necessitating the building of a stockade on Johnson's Island in Lake Erie. Most of the officers imprisoned at Camp Chase were transferred to Johnson's Island once the stockade was completed.

During the smallpox epidemic of 1863, some five hundred of the imprisoned soldiers died in the month of February alone. Overcrowding forced two or three men to share single bunks and led to severe shortages in food, medicine, clothing, and blankets. Malnourished and cold, the men were highly susceptible to disease.

The prison stockade at Camp Chase, from an 1861 sketch.

Near the end of that deadly year, a cemetery was built at the camp. As a result, the Confederate dead who had been buried in the city cemetery were moved back to Camp Chase and buried under cheap wooden markers in a plot surrounded by a low fence.

When the war ended in 1865, most of Camp Chase itself was dismantled. Some of the cabins where POWs had been housed were used as shanties for a few years; but for the most part, every trace of Camp Chase would soon be gone—except for the graveyard, which was left to deteriorate until it was restored and used as a gathering place for patriotic speeches in the 1890s.

Today the small cemetery is picturesque and well maintained, its wooden headstones replaced with granite. Its centerpiece is an arch constructed from granite blocks. Atop the arch stands the statue of a Confederate soldier facing south, and on the keystone below his feet is engraved a single word: AMERICANS.

✸ **Camp Chase Confederate Cemetery, 2900 Sullivant Ave., Columbus, OH 43204, (937) 262-2115, www.cem.va.gov/cems/ lots/campchase.asp; open Mon.–Fri., 8 a.m.–4:30 p.m.**

A photograph of the memorial arch taken soon after it was unveiled in 1902.

The gravestone of Private Benjamin F. Allen, over which the Lady in Gray is said to weep.

WHO'S THAT LADY?

So many men died miserably here at a young age that it's surprising the Lady in Gray is the only ghost who haunts the place. She is described by witnesses as wearing a flowing gray dress and a gray veil hiding her face. Is she Benjamin Allen's Tennessee bride, weeping over the reunion that never happened?

Visitors to the cemetery and even those passing by the gates have reported seeing this woman walking among the seemingly endless line of tombstones. Once in a while, she is even seen walking through the locked cemetery gates at night. But more often than not, she is spotted standing over two specific graves— that of Benjamin Allen and one of an unknown soldier.

Researchers of the paranormal have yet to figure out who the ghostly woman is and why she chooses to mourn where she does. She doesn't appear to be the spirit of any known relative of Mr. Allen's, and her concern for an unknown soldier further compounds the mystery. Perhaps the Lady in Gray isn't connected to these graves at all but is simply eternally mourning the atrocities of war in general.

A HAUNTING COLLECTION ☞ *Linda S. Godfrey*

For Civil War buff and collector Michael Wozny, the two-story frame house just off the historic downtown square in East Troy, WI, fulfilled all the requirements of his dream home. Wozny and his wife, Sherry, needed a vintage place to display their Civil War uniforms and artifacts, and the Greek Revival, wood-floored house built on one of the oldest home sites in Walworth County still looked much the same as when it was built in 1857 by Dr. Levi Stebbins. What the Woznys didn't realize, however, was that Dr. Stebbins—and perhaps others among the nine inhabitants who died in that home—might never have left.

The Woznys began noticing strange things soon after they moved in. An antique, tin camping cup kept on the living room mantel tended to hop around by itself, for instance. Michael got eerie feelings while sitting in his office at the end of the downstairs hallway, and one day he turned to catch a glimpse of a man dressed in what looked like a Civil War–era frock coat.

The Woznys decided to research the home's history and discovered their dream house had a dark background.

THE LONG CHAIN OF DEATH

First to die was an infant—the seventh child of Levi and Sabrena Stebbins. Their daughter died a few days after birth in August 1857, just a few months after the family had moved in. The baby's funeral was held in the front parlor of the house.

The second person to die was a Stebbins son, who was run over by a stagecoach. He was carried into the house, where he expired despite his father's desperate effort to save him. Daughter Laurie passed away elsewhere at age thirty-one in 1869, but hers was the house's third funeral. She was followed in death by her father, the doctor, who died in 1881 in his bed from pneumonia. Like his children, he was laid in state in the parlor. His wife, Sabrena, was the fourth person to die in the house, in 1887.

The next year, retired farmer Richard Brownlee bought the Stebbins estate and moved in with his son, David, and two daughters, Susan and Martha ("Mittie"). Richard died in his bed on October 9, 1907, and his funeral was held in the residence soon after. His children (David, d. 1934; Mittie, d. 1941; and Susan, d. 1942) became the sixth through eighth persons to shuck their mortal coils in the old house on Main Street. ☞

☞ "Wozny also began having eerie problems with the tin Civil War field cup. 'I'd leave the room and come back and find it sitting on the middle of the table,' he said. 'So I put it on the bookshelf. The next day it was completely gone, then I found it the following day inside a cabinet used to store other Civil War items, pushed in next to them.'"

A ca. 1862 hand-colored tintype of an unidentified Union soldier in a black coat, with his tin cup, similar to the one in Michael Wozny's collection.

Susan willed the house to her nephew, Ralph Brownlee, who in turn sold the place to a brother, George, and his two sisters, Alma Lazzaroni and Genevieve Cruver, who all managed to survive three years in the house before selling it in 1946. Perhaps they had good reason for moving, with eight possible revenants already on the property. The house changed hands a few more times in the next couple of years, and the ninth and final death occurred in 1954, when Mrs. Josephine Feuerpfeil succumbed to a heart attack in the master bedroom.

A succession of several more owners and tenants lived in the house of death before the Woznys bought it in 1996.

PHANTOM HITCHHIKER

According to Michael Wozny, it's possible that the chief spook on the premises, the man in the black frock coat, didn't pass away in the East Troy house. The shadow man may have hitched a ride with the Civil War memorabilia Wozny collected from all over the country. Wozny lived in an apartment with his antique paraphernalia for some time before meeting Sherry, he said, and at least two women he dated described seeing "something" that looked like a man in a long full coat and short-brimmed hat. When he met Sherry, she described the same thing.

Wozny also began having eerie problems with the tin Civil War field cup. "I'd leave the room and come back and find it sitting on the middle of the table," he said. "So I put it on the bookshelf. The next day it was completely gone, then I found it the following day inside a cabinet used to store other Civil War items, pushed in next to them."

The cup disappeared yet again, reappearing in the cabinet only when Wozny removed the other items that had been "crowding" it. The cup stayed quiet until the Halloween after the Woznys moved into their East Troy house, when it again "apported"—a term for the unknown means by which objects vanish and return on their own—by disappearing from the mantel and ending up on the windowsill.

Although Wozny never saw the man in the black frock coat while living in his apartment, he soon encountered the shadowy being when he and Sherry moved into the old Stebbins House. It was after the Halloween incident, about a year after they had moved in, and Wozny was sitting alone in his library, working. "I suddenly looked up and saw a black figure in the middle of the room," said Wozny. "It was like a shadow, only you couldn't see through it, and it was in the room itself—not on the wall. It had a long coat and a short, 'preacher's' hat. I started to get up and it turned to move away, breaking up into some twinkly stuff."

Wozny says he was surprised but not shaken. From time to time after that incident, he would catch glimpses of the figure out of the corner of his eye. "It was like a shadow person walking across the room, but not on the wall," he said.

HALF BOY AND OTHER GHOSTS

In February 2008, Wozny spotted another figure—half a boy! A TV had broken, and he had moved it to the floor and left it there until he could get it out of the house. One day when he walked into the room, he saw the bottom half of what looked like a boy or young man wearing blue pants and black shoes and sitting on the TV. The figure trailed off into vapor above the belt. As Wozny came into the room, the legs stood up and walked away.

Wozny also had a strange experience while trying to drag a heavy board up the narrow stairs inside the property's two-story carriage house. He was having a difficult time of it, when suddenly it was as if someone picked up the other end and took most of the load. "It felt light as a feather," said Wozny. "I just said, 'Thank you, whoever you are.' That was weird."

There have been other incidents. A former upstairs tenant said he saw a figure he thought might be Dr. Stebbins standing in the hall. In the tenant's bedroom, the former master bedroom where several occupants died, the closet door would not stay shut—even when heavy objects were placed in front of it.

Wozny said that for some time, he was repeatedly awakened at night by someone insistently tapping one of his feet. It ended when he firmly asked the unknown tapper to stop it. And around Christmas of 2007, Mike and Sherry took some pictures of their front porch, only to discover the image of a lady in a white dress standing inside, looking out at them.

Despite all of this, the Woznys are not planning to move. Nothing much surprises them anymore, and they say they have no problem sharing their home with the mostly unseen inhabitants. After all, what could be more appropriate for a man who used to spend all his free time reenacting the Civil War, than hosting the spirits of those who actually lived it?

✳ **This historic house is a private residence.**

THE MAN OF THE HOUSE ☞ *Steven LaChance*

Do you believe in ghosts? I used to be like most people—a true skeptic, a real disbeliever. That was until a few years ago. Now I do believe, and I wish I didn't. Even now, I'm awakened in the night by the memory of the screaming man and the dark ghostly image that turned my world upside down.

It was May 2001, and as a single father with three children, I desperately needed to find a place for my family to live. The lease on our apartment was up and we were about to find ourselves homeless. I had answered just about every Union, MO, for-rent ad when I received a call from a woman telling me about a house she owned—a rather large old place, she said, that was in very good shape. She invited me to an open house that coming Sunday.

When Sunday rolled around and my daughter and I arrived at the house, we could barely believe our eyes. We gazed upward in the living room to see cherubs lining the top of the wallpaper. All of the original woodwork was intact, and a wooden partition separated the living room from the huge family room. Just as amazing, the smell of baking cookies had hit us as soon as we walked through the front door.

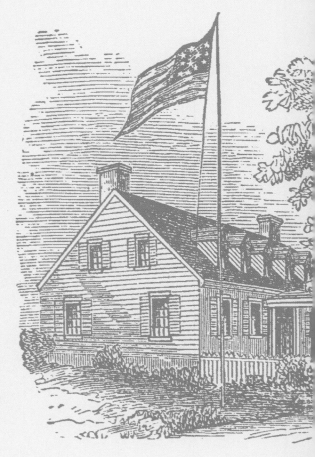

The house had two floors, three bedrooms, and a large family kitchen with a mudroom that led to the back door. Upstairs, a breezeway was accessible to both bedrooms, and the basement had been used as a fruit cellar. It was more house than we ever imagined for the price, and we immediately knew we had to have it. Anyone who has lived in an apartment with three children will understand how we felt.

There was a steady stream of potential renters at the open house, so we knew the competition would be tough. I asked the elderly landlady if I could fill out the rental application on the spot, and she immediately agreed. As I handed her my application, she asked, "Do you understand the responsibility that comes with living in an old house such as this?"

"Oh yes, I understand. It's beautiful," I quickly replied, never imagining what lay in store. "Well then, I'll get back to you," she said before walking off to attend to other visitors. I couldn't help but notice that there was something a little odd about the woman, and the way she showed people around wasn't typical of real estate agents. She showed the house as if it were a museum.

> ☞ "I was hanging a large picture of two angels in the living room . . . . Finished, I turned to walk away. Then crash! The picture fell to the floor. I rehung it and turned away, only for it to fall again. After I hung it a third time and walked away, I felt a rush of air hit the back of my ankles."

A week or so later, the landlady called to tell me she had selected me as the renter. While I was thrilled, I was surprised to find her downright effusive. We agreed to meet the following day at a restaurant not far from my workplace to settle all of the paperwork and take care of the deposit and initial monthly payment. I was a little disappointed we wouldn't be meeting at the house because I couldn't wait to see it again — and, in fact, meeting in a restaurant seemed just as off-kilter as the landlady's sudden excitement.

Why worry about something so minor, I asked myself, when we'd lucked into such an incredible deal? I signed the papers just as planned the next day, and the children and I were all set to move in at the end of that week — Memorial Day weekend.

MOVING PICTURES, FALLING LEAVES

It seemed forever before moving day finally came; but once it did, we quickly got all of our belongings stored safely inside the old white house. I was hauling the last few items from the moving truck when a passing car slowed to a crawl. From the passenger side, a man leaned out the window and said, "Hope you get along okay here," before the car sped up and drove away.

"What do you think of that, Dad?" my daughter asked, slightly puzzled. "Friendly neighbors," I replied as I shut the sliding door of the truck.

The first night in the house passed uneventfully. Looking back, I wonder if that might have been because the house wanted to draw us in a little closer before beginning its series of assaults. However, I did notice something strange. Each of the interior doors had an old hook-and-eye latch, but not in the usual place. The latches were outside the doors, as if to keep something in.

A few days later, the first incident occurred. I was hanging a large picture of two angels in the living room after my daughter suggested it would complement the cherubs lining the ceiling. Finished, I turned to walk away. Then crash! The picture fell to the floor. I rehung it and turned away, only for it to fall again. After I hung it a third time and walked away, I felt a rush of air hit the back of my ankles.

"What the hell?" I thought. I turned to see the picture lying at my feet. More determined than ever, I hung the picture again, then shouted, "Stay there, dammit." I had to laugh because I was alone. Who did I think I was talking to? The kids were out playing on the front porch.

"Dad, come and see this," my daughter called from the front door. ☞

When I stepped onto the porch, she said excitedly, "Sit down and watch this!"

"Watch what?"

Just as the words came out of my mouth, my daughter pointed to an old man walking down the sidewalk toward our house. When he reached our property line, he quickly crossed the street to the opposite sidewalk.

"They don't like walking in front of our house," said my daughter. "Isn't that weird?" And she was right. I sat on that porch for at least an hour, watching our neighbors cross the street. A couple of times I motioned as if to say hello, and they just dropped their heads and continued on their way. "Maybe they're uncomfortable with new neighbors," I thought, though in my heart I knew otherwise.

That Sunday, the kids returned from church excited because we had set aside the whole day to work in the yard—a big deal, since the only outdoor space they had ever been able to call theirs was the balcony outside our old apartment. We mowed the grass and cleaned the leaves from under the porch. We also needed to rake the lawn because the trees were shedding their leaves— even though it was spring, not fall. I made a mental note to mention this oddity to the landlady the next time I talked with her.

I asked my younger son to go inside and down to the basement to fetch the garden hose so we could clean the walkways and wash down the house's weathered white boards. Only a minute or two passed before I heard screams, and I ran in frantically to find him. He was standing in the middle of the kitchen floor shaking, a puddle of urine at his feet.

"What's wrong? What happened?" I asked.

"Something chased me up the basement steps."

"What chased you?" I asked.

"I don't know, Daddy, but it was big."

My other two children and I checked the basement and found only the garden hose that my youngest had dropped in fear.

THE MAN IN THE MIST

Aside from this strange incident, we were incredibly happy those first few days in the house. My daughter was making plans for gardening and decorating, and my boys realized it would be easy to walk to their baseball games because the park was so close by. But this uneventful time wouldn't last for long.

It was the children's last week of classes, and that Monday we all arrived after school and work to find every light in the house switched on. My first impulse was to blame the children, who pleaded innocence. The same thing happened on Tuesday, Wednesday, and Thursday. On Friday, my daughter and I sent the boys to the car while we purposely toured the house looking for any forgotten lights. They were all off.

That night, we returned home to again find every light burning. I walked into the house feeling shaken. The only logical explanation for the lights being on was that someone was in our house. I searched the rooms in a panic, but found no one.

"Daddy, it's cold in here," my daughter called from the living room. What was she talking about? Sweat was pouring down my back. I stepped into the living room, and the temperature dropped what seemed a good thirty degrees. More ominously, I felt a presence. I didn't see anything, but what felt like an electrical current ran through my body and gave me goose bumps. I remember thinking, "What on earth was that?"

Now my daughter remarked, "Daddy, it's getting warm in here." And sure enough, the temperature was rising. That night my children slept with me, though I got hardly any sleep.

The following Sunday night, we were sitting in the family room talking. The kids had their backs to the kitchen—something I'm still thankful for, since what happened next haunts my dreams to this day.

I was getting ready to take a business trip the following morning to Indianapolis, and the children and I were watching TV and discussing the plans for their stay at Grandma's. I noticed it first out of the corner of my eye: something moving, then standing in the kitchen doorway. Not something, really— someone. I looked toward it again to see the dark figure of a man. Though he was human in shape, his body looked like a mass of churning black mist or smoke, and I heard heavy, labored breathing. I looked down, thinking my eyes were playing tricks on me.

After a moment passed, I looked up. He was still there and began to move into the room. The churning black form stood in the doorway for what seemed an eternity but was actually only a few moments. He then melted into thin air.

I remember the thoughts that raced through my head; I have two choices. We could run out of the house screaming into the night or we could get up and quietly leave the house and figure all of this out.

My hands shook uncontrollably as I said to myself, *That's what we'll do. We'll go quietly, orderly, as if nothing was wrong.* I stood up shakily, and in my nicest, calmest daddy voice said, "Let's go get a soda and see Grandma." My youngest was instantly excited at the prospect of a soda before bed, but the two others looked at me as if I'd lost my mind. "Come on guys, it'll be fun."

> **☛ "I noticed it first out of the corner of my eye: something moving, then standing in the kitchen doorway. Not something, really— someone. Though he was human in shape, his body looked like a mass of churning black mist or smoke, and I heard heavy, labored breathing."**

Thankfully, my car keys were on the coffee table in front of us, and we moved in an orderly fashion out the front door. As I turned to lock it, the painful wail of a man welled up from inside, so loud that the neighborhood dogs began barking.

To hell with orderly, I thought. "Get in the car!" The drive to my parents' house is still a blur. I do remember that my younger son, who was trembling with fright, said, "Daddy, the basement monster is standing in the upstairs window." I looked back—and sure enough, the black form was in the window, watching us leave.

That night we stayed at my parents'. Early the next day, I gathered my things and left for my business trip. By the time I got back and picked up the kids, I had a whole week's worth of rationalizations for why we should return to the house. Where else were we to go? I had put everything I had saved and then some into the move. We returned that Friday, and to my relief the weekend passed without incident—not to mention very little sleep.

On Saturday, we explored the big shed at the back of the yard. In it we found personal belongings that clearly had belonged to several different people. This raised a question: Who had lived in the house before, and what might that explain?

THE TERRIBLE ENCOUNTER

My parents agreed that it would be a good idea for me to call the old landlady and ask her some straightforward questions about the house and its ☛

former occupants. Once I was able to reach her, I chose my words carefully and asked in my most polite voice whether any of the previous tenants had ever perhaps mentioned a ghost?

She answered, "Not that I can remember." She then said that there had been one strange tenant: a girl who claimed that her dead father came to visit her, but the old woman always thought she was crazy. The girl had left some of her stuff behind in the shed, but the landlady could never get her to come pick it up.

The other belongings were those of a man who had lived there and had left in the middle of the night, taking nothing. But, no, she had never heard of anyone talking about the house being haunted. I asked how long these people had lived there, and she replied, "Not much more than a year. Why do you ask?" The phone call wasn't much help. And it didn't calm my fears much, but what else could I do?

Sunday came and went with no trouble, and I was convincing myself that what we had gone through was just a one-time ordeal. But everything changed on Monday night. I was on the phone with my mom, and the kids were off playing in my bedroom. Suddenly, the doors inside the house rattled. I paused to listen, and they rattled again. I yelled at the kids to quit playing games and told my mom that everything was okay—just the kids playing tricks. At this point the doors rattled more loudly, but before I could scold again, my daughter's voice cut me off.

"Daddy, I'm in here reading and my brothers are asleep."

I will now try to recreate what happened as best I can. Some of it I remember clearly, but other parts are not clear to this day.

The temperature instantly dropped thirty degrees and I felt a terrible shiver run through my body. A horrible stench filled the air, and then the screaming started: softly at first, then growing louder. I shouted into the phone to my mother that she had to drive to our street and meet us at the top of the hill.

Now the whole house began to shake. From above I could hear something large coming down the stairs (Boom. Boom! BOOM!) . . . the screaming of a man, over and over . . . and my daughter screaming, "Daddy, what is happening?" One of my two bedroom doors led to the stairs, and I had to rescue my children!

The floor beneath me was shaking as I made my way to the opposite bedroom door. I felt something behind me but didn't want to turn around. When I made it to the door, it wouldn't open. Screaming myself by this time, I threw myself against the door, but it wouldn't budge. I tried again and again until it flew open. I told my older son to get his brother and run out the front door to the car, but my shocked daughter wouldn't move. A slap made her respond, and I grabbed her and headed for the door as I heard the other bedroom door open behind us. Whatever it was, it was coming for us. After we ran out onto the porch, I slammed the front door behind us.

As we jumped into the car, we could still hear the angry noises coming from the house. I sped away and parked at the top of the street, where I could look down into the house and wait for my parents. My children and I could see something through the windows: a blackness moving methodically through the house from room to room. It seemed to be searching—searching for us! That was our last night in the house, and my children never returned.

I went back a few times to collect our belongings, but never alone. Anyone who accompanied me would experience something strange—a scream, whispers, pounding from the floor above. One day while I was down in the dim basement, my brother snapped a picture of me. I can't say why, but perhaps after all I'd told him about the house and its spooky basement he just wanted to document my brief stay there—or maybe so that he could kid me about it for years to come.

Nobody joked around, however, after we developed the photo and saw the cloudy image of a man standing behind me in a darkened corner of the cellar. Though shadowy, the figure was clear enough for us to make out some details. The man seemed to be from a different time, with old-fashioned clothes and a bow tie. His face was a very angry one.

About a month after we moved, my brother sent me an e-mail with a link to a website that he desperately wanted me to see. He said he had been doing some poking around online, looking into local history, when he found something that made his jaw drop. I went to the site he gave me, and the face of a man came onto my screen—the same face that showed up in the picture my brother had taken in the basement.

The man, Brevet Major General Eugene Asa Carr, was apparently quite well known as a Civil War officer—a hero, in fact. He was also a very well-respected town citizen in his day and had once owned the house and surrounding land that my kids and I had fled from in the night. Still, there was nothing on the Internet that could explain why he might still be in the house or why he would want everyone else out of it.

EPILOGUE

About a year ago, an acquaintance of mine saw a police car race up to the old house one night, and then watched a family running out of the front door in their nightclothes. After that, the old lady turned the place into a dog kennel. I guess she ran out of people who could live in that old white house.

I still drive past it every once in a while when I get up enough nerve. As I look up at the upstairs window, I can still imagine "the man of the house" there—

Brevet Major General Eugene Asa Carr, ca. 1864.

watching, waiting, angry. Sometimes the screams still wake me from my sleep. In my dreams I see a man standing in the basement, breathing. It's the breathing I'd hear when I was alone with him in a room. The breathing I'd hear that let me know he was there with me—heavy, labored breathing.

I remember what the old landlady said to me as I turned over the key after we moved out. The side of my arm was still bruised from throwing myself against that bedroom door that last night in the house. "Some people are meant to live in an old house like that," she told me, "and some people aren't. I never thought you were the old-house type." And I know now that she was right.

✳ **This historic house is a private residence.**

 CHAPTER NINE

THE PLAINS
AND
SOUTHWEST

NEW MEXICO, OKLAHOMA & TEXAS

LEGALLY DEAD: A HAUNTED D.A.'S OFFICE ☞ *Gloria McCary*

The county-owned building that formerly housed the D.A.'s office is on the southern end of what was the Plaza Mayor of the ancient settlement of Socorro, NM. It's a long, relatively narrow, nondescript adobe building but is recognizable in photos of Socorro taken in the 1880s. I went to work in this building as a deputy district attorney in March 2001.

About two months into my employment, the first incident occurred. Our investigator, Juanita, was walking back from the restroom to the front of the building when she heard my voice calling her name. When she walked into my office, she was surprised to find it empty. Seated in a nearby cubicle, my secretary, Virginia, said, "I heard it, too, but Gloria's been in court all morning."

A few months later, I was standing in the secretarial area speaking with Bella, the chief deputy D.A.'s secretary. Behind me I could hear Susan, another secretary, typing busily at her computer. I turned around to say something to Susan and found that not only was her workstation empty, but her computer was turned off. I turned back to Bella and said, "I swear I heard Susan working on her computer."

Bella laughed and said, "Susan's out sick today, but her computer has been typing all morning, even though no one's turned it on." We began discussing the invisible typist, and Bella, who often worked late into the night, said, "I always keep my radio on when I'm in here alone. That way I can't hear the weird noises. I've never seen anything, though. I just hear the noises."

A year or so later, Bruce, the chief deputy district attorney, was in the men's room when the top paper towel of the stack on the toilet tank suddenly rose straight up into the air, turned ninety degrees, floated a couple of inches toward him, and dropped to the floor. About six months after Bruce's experience, I was preparing for a vehicular homicide trial with another lawyer named Nikki when we distinctly heard Virginia come back from lunch and resume work, rolling her chair back and forth on its carpet-saver pad as she shuffled papers and moved files. Neither Nikki nor I could remember if an important witness in the trial had been subpoenaed. "Virginia will know," I said, jumping up from the desk and opening the door.

In fact, Virginia was still at lunch.

*Previous page*s: A Confederate soldier on top of a rebel look-out tower, Bolivar Point, Galveston Island, TX, ca. 1863. The Confederates recaptured the key port city of Galveston from the Union in January 1863 and held it until the end of the war.

UNEARTHING THE PAST

Though no one has actually seen a ghost in the office, most of us have heard mysterious shuffling, typing, and other strange noises over the years. The cause of this ghoulish racket is unknown, but examining the site's history provides a few possibilities.

The area around Socorro was originally settled by Native Americans, followed in 1598 by Spanish colonists. The natives of nearby Teypana provided the struggling European settlers with food and water and the colonists later renamed the pueblo Socorro to commemorate the natives' succor, or help. However, relations between the native pueblos of New Mexico and their Spanish rulers became strained, resulting in the Pueblo Revolt of 1680. Many colonists were killed.

It is unknown when the current law office structure was built, but the building served the famous lawman Elfego Baca and was a tuberculosis hospital and even a combination brothel-saloon during Socorro's wild and woolly days in the mid- and late nineteenth century. With such a long and varied history, the premises could have been the setting for any number of demises. There were certainly deaths during the building's years as a tuberculosis clinic, and probably more when it was a saloon and brothel and full of cattlemen and miners who were dry after a dusty day's work.

In February 1862, wounded soldiers from the Civil War battle of Valverde were transported to Socorro for medical treatment. They were housed near the central plaza, though it's unknown which buildings were used as field hospitals.

The most obvious explanation for the law office hauntings, however, can be traced to a fairly recent tragedy. A decade or so prior to my tenure there, a secretary had been disturbed by serious health problems, which impelled her to retire from the office and later commit suicide. Bruce believes that the unhappy woman has returned to her former workplace indefinitely, carrying out the duties she was unable to complete in life.

The D.A.'s office has since moved across the street to a more modern, 1930s-era building.

⊛ **Fort Craig Historic Site is located 35 miles south of Socorro, NM; see website for directions and map, www.blm.gov/nm/st/en/prog/recreation/socorro/ fort_craig.html. Open year-round during daylight hours.**

The ruins of Fort Craig, a fortification built by the U.S. Army in 1854 near Socorro, NM, and employed as a Union outpost during the Civil War. The Battle of Valverde, the largest Civil War battle in the Southwest, was fought on February 20–21, 1862, upstream from Fort Craig at Valverde Crossing. Wounded soldiers from the battle were brought to Socorro for treatment—perhaps those who did not survive linger on to this day?

THE TRI-STATE SPOOK LIGHT

Judging from the stories dating back to nineteenth-century Oklahoma, you'd think that one in every five relationships ended with one person killing the other, that the most common cause of death among settlers was decapitation, and that pioneers went looking for things only in the dead of night. Then again, tales of mild-mannered townsfolk who ran feed stores and died uneventfully of old age in their beds don't usually get passed down through the generations.

Without these fantastic narratives, we might not have anything to talk about as we slouch in our car seats on darkened back roads waiting for mysterious dancing lights to make an appearance—a popular activity with people living in northeast Oklahoma. This is, after all, the location of the Spooksville Triangle,

a region famous for unusual nighttime phenomena. Stretching between Miami, OK; Columbus, KS; and Joplin, MO, the region is rife with unexplained lights that taunt visitors and elude rational explanation.

The most famous of these luminous entities is the Tri-State Spook Light, which actually lies just outside the designated triangle along East 50 Road, just this side of the Oklahoma–Missouri state line. Locals say that if you park your car about a half-mile west of the border and face the Show-Me State, you'll see a show you'll never forget.

According to witnesses, the light emerges from the trees along the shoulder and floats out above the roadway. It always appears as an orb, but varies in both size and color, usually measuring from somewhere about the size of a volleyball to as much as five feet

in diameter. Sometimes the light will change in both size and color right before your eyes, apparently depending on its mood. On occasion, multiple orbs will even appear together, dancing and leap-frogging like puppies in a pet-shop window.

The phenomenon is typically shy, though, and will dart off if you honk your car horn or turn on your headlights. Yet some allege to have encountered the light up close when it approached their vehicles as though suddenly curious about its audience. A few have said the light even entered their cars, at which point the astonished passengers felt an intense warmth radiating from the orb. In one case, the light hitched a ride on a school bus taking kids home from a carnival, jumping out when it apparently reached its destination.

The earliest verifiable report of the light dates back to 1936, but many claim that locals have known about it as far back as the mid-1800s. Native Americans may have been aware of it even further back than that. As such, numerous legends have attached themselves to the phenomenon. In one case, a young girl was said to have been lost at night while looking for stray cows. Her mother, who searched for her by the light of a lantern, was so upset by the loss that she continues her search in the afterlife. In another story, the lantern is said to belong to a prospector who was decapitated in a mining accident. Another recounts the tale of a soldier whose head was blown off by a cannon ball during the Civil War. Then there's the Seneca Indian who got into an argument with his ax-wielding wife and—you guessed it—lost his head. A more romantic version of the story tells of two Indian lovers who were unable to marry and leaped to their deaths. They continue to seek each other nightly.

Naturally, many people have attempted to explain the lights scientifically. In the 1940s, the U.S. Army Corps of Engineers came to have a look, as did a scientist from the Midwest Research Institute in Kansas City, MOG. In 1969, a professor from ☛

> ☛ "In another story, the lantern is said to belong to a prospector who was decapitated in a mining accident. Another recounts the tale of a soldier whose head was blown off by a cannon ball during the Civil War."

Opposite left and *above*: Old photographs that captured the mysterious Tri-State Spook Light; is it the ghost of a decapitated Civil War soldier with a lantern forever searching for his head?

Southwest Missouri State University performed his own study. In the years since, numerous scientists, ufologists, and documentarians have conducted investigations with varying levels of scrutiny and technical expertise. No one has come up with a conclusive answer for the light.

That's not to say that myriad theories haven't been proposed, of course. Swamp gas is a popular one, as is static electricity. Some are convinced that mineral deposits are at the root. Ball lightning, plasma, and natural phosphorescence round out the more far-reaching explanations. More often than not, though, skeptics insist that it's just the result of distant car headlights refracted by the atmosphere, although that doesn't explain the reports that originated before the advent of headlighted vehicles.

Regardless, it seems the light doesn't stick to one spot. In addition to East 50 Road, otherwise known as Devil's Promenade, reports indicate that you're likely to catch it playing to the north over on East 40 Road,

as well. You might also catch it at Devil's Promenade Bridge to the west, where East 57 crosses Spring River, especially when the Quapaw tribe holds their annual powwow nearby. However, East 50 remains the most popular viewing area and the one most everyone will point you to when asked.

When inquiring about directions, though, don't be surprised if the locals correct you on the name. "Tri-State Spook Light" is more the phenomenon's politically correct moniker, as multiple towns in three different states claim the spectacle as their own. In Missouri, you might hear it called the Hornet Spook Light, the Neosho Spook Light, the Seneca Spook Light, or the Joplin Spook Light. Kansans say it's appeared on their side of the state line, also. In Oklahoma, the towns of Quapaw, Miami, and Peoria have all staked naming rights, so you might as well call it what you want.

✳ **The Tri-State Spook Light is sometimes visible on the E. 50 Rd., just this side of the Oklahoma–Missouri state line.**

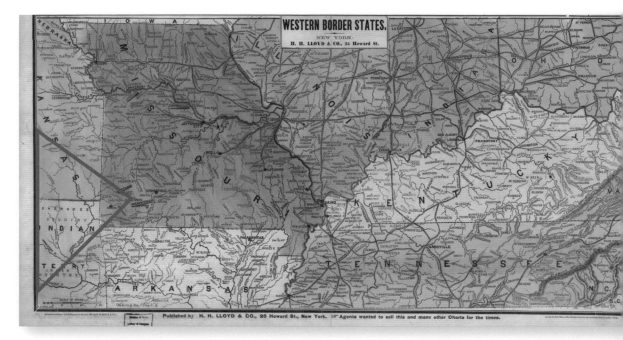

A map from ca. 1861 depicting the Western border states. Oklahoma, at the time part of the Indian Territory, is shown at bottom left. The "Spooksville Triangle" region is roughly indicated by the red triangle drawn on the map.

Spook Light Spotting Is a Family Affair

My mother was raised in northeast Oklahoma during the Depression. Most summers in the early 1960s she and I and my older brother would venture up there from Texas. Even when I was little, I remember all of us driving out of Fairland, OK, to this deserted country road where we would sit for hours waiting for the Spook Light to appear. There were the usual explanations: swamp gas, car lights refracted somewhere, and so on. My mother told us her father used to see it when he was a kid, before cars were invented. His generation believed the Spook Light had something to do with lost and wandering Cherokee spirits. Others claimed it was the ghost of a Civil War soldier with a lantern, out looking for his decapitated head.

My favorite story involved a couple of policemen who witnessed the light come close enough to pounce on the hood of their patrol car, then the trunk, before disappearing.

Most of the time, I remember falling asleep in the car, waiting and waiting, then waking up on the way home, my mother telling me if they had seen the light or not. Finally, one night when I was about six, I got to see it for myself; it was exactly as everyone had described it to me over the years. It started out way down the road, and it took a while to get your eyes focused on it. What was cool was hearing other car doors opening and realizing about five or six other families had come out there late on a summer evening for the same thing.

I was frightened at first, but that faded as the phantom light came closer and more focused in intensity. I could see why some people described it as the front light on an approaching train. Except as a train light grows in intensity and illumination, it also increases its circumference, which helps you to keep it in perspective as to its proximity. The Spook Light, however, grew only in illuminated intensity; it never grew in size. It consistently appeared to be the size of a bowling ball.

This first time I saw it was cool because I really thought this thing would dance or bounce around like I had always heard. I wasn't disappointed, because the closer it got, the more you could see that it wasn't taking an entirely straight course; it veered and dipped ever so slightly.

As my family and I watched it approach, I heard the excitement of the other families around us, particularly the random *boo*, and the high shrill squeak from some poor little kid, followed by laughter. But I didn't take my eyes off the Spook Light. What happened next was the part that made that night even more memorable.

The light just veered off to its left in a wide arc, cutting across a field, but fast, like a big round rocket hitting a booster stage, and BOOM. Everyone sort of oohed and aahed together when that happened. It was the only time I observed the light seeming to change in its size and intensity as it faded off. I did see it other times later, but it was never as cool as the first time. ~*Nick Beef*

THE SECRET LIFE OF JOHN WILKES BOOTH

The date was April 14, 1865. The War Between the States was nearly at an end, with Robert E. Lee having formally surrendered to Ulysses S. Grant just five days earlier. President Abraham Lincoln, who was in good spirits, celebrated the excellent news by accepting an invitation to a play.

Of course, anyone who's made it through fifth-grade social studies knows what happened next. John Wilkes Booth, actor and Confederate sympathizer, made his way into Lincoln's theater box and shot the president in the back of the head with a single-shot derringer pistol (see also pages 114–15).

Booth had counted on a quick getaway, but had trouble when he leapt from the box and clumsily caught his riding spur on a U.S. Treasury Guards flag, tumbling to the stage and breaking his leg. Nevertheless, after shouting that infamous cry, "*Sic semper tyrannis*!"—the Virginia state motto meaning "Thus always to tyrants"—Booth ran outside, mounted the horse that was waiting for him, and rendezvoused with fellow conspirator David Herold in Maryland.

After staying the night with acquaintance Dr. Samuel Mudd, who reset Booth's broken leg, Booth and Herold fled for Virginia, where they were discovered several days later hiding out in a barn. Surrounded by Union soldiers in the early morning hours, Herold surrendered, but Booth stood his ground. As the soldiers began setting fire to the barn, a sergeant named Boston Corbett spotted Booth through a gap in a wall and fired at him, striking him in the back of the neck. Booth succumbed to his wound a few hours later and was eventually buried in a family plot in Baltimore, Maryland. (Cue the suspenseful music.) Or was he?

A broadside issued by the war department on April 20, 1865, advertising a reward for the capture of the Lincoln assassination conspirators.

The .44-caliber derringer pistol that John Wilkes Booth used to change American history.

BOOTH.   HAROLD.

artment, Washington, April 20, 1865,

00,000 REWARD!

MURDERER

eloved President, Abraham Lincoln,

STILL AT LARGE.

000 REWARD

Department for his apprehension, in addition to any reward offered by
r State Executives.

000 REWARD

apprehension of JOHN H. SURRATT, one of Booth's Accomplices.

000 REWARD

apprehension of David C. Harold, another of Booth's accomplices.

will be paid for any information that shall conduce to the arrest of either of the above-
mplices.

secreting the said persons, or either of them, or aiding or assisting their concealment or
mplices in the murder of the President and the attempted assassination of the Secretary of
rial before a Military Commission and the punishment of DEATH.
blood be removed from the land by the arrest and punishment of the murderers.
rted to aid public justice on this occasion. Every man should consider his own conscience
and rest neither night nor day until it be accomplished.

EDWIN M. STANTON, Secretary of War.

TH is Five Feet 7 or 8 inches high, slender build, high forehead, black hair, black eyes, and

out 5 feet, 9 inches. Hair rather thin and dark; eyes rather light; no beard. Would
complexion rather pale and clear, with color in his cheeks. Wore light clothes of fine
hook bones rather prominent; chin narrow; ears projecting at the top; forehead rather
arts his hair on the right side; neck rather long. His lips are firmly set. A slim man.
five feet six inches high, hair dark, eyes dark, eyebrows rather heavy, full face, nose short,
all, instep high, round, bodied, naturally quick and active, slightly closes his eyes when

the above, State and other authorities have offered rewards amounting to almost one hun-
an aggregate of about TWO HUNDRED THOUSAND DOLLARS.

ALIAS DAVID GEORGE

Thirty-eight years later, a man by the name of David E. George would raise doubt concerning the fate of Lincoln's assassin. In January 1903, in a long narrow room on an upstairs floor of the Grand Avenue Hotel in Enid, OK, George made a startling confession. He was dying, and although a doctor had been called to his bedside, there was nothing the physician could do; George had ingested a fatal dose of strychnine. As the dying man drew his last breath, he confessed that David George was just an alias. His real name was John Wilkes Booth, and he had killed Abraham Lincoln (see also pages 65–67).

None of the locals really seemed to know that much about George. He was a self-professed house painter and devoted barfly, that much they could say—though he was fond of quoting Shakespeare, which he did at length when he was on the drink, which raised speculation that he may have once been very familiar with the stage. Was it possible that he was who he claimed to be?

The evidence began to pile up. Upon examination of George's body, doctors noticed scars that matched those Booth would have had. He had also suffered a broken leg sometime in the past, just above the ankle, as Booth had when he leaped to the stage at Ford's Theatre. Plus, he shared Booth's height and features, and was of the proper age. Moreover, a minister by the name of E. D. Harper revealed that, during a previous suicide attempt, George had confessed once before to being Booth.

Still, nothing came of the matter. And since no one came forward to claim the body, the local mortician mummified George, dressed him up, and set him on display in the front window of his funeral parlor/furniture store. Despite George's supposedly astonishing revelation, he remained little more than a minor curiosity.

The mystery grew, however, when Finis L. Bates, a lawyer from Memphis, heard about George's claim, traveled to Enid to see the corpse for himself, and identified it as the man he once knew as John St. Helen. St. Helen, he said, had been a friend of his back when he worked in Granbury, TX in the 1870s. Furthermore, at a time when St. Helen was gravely ill and believed he was lying on his deathbed, he confessed to Bates that he was the man who killed Lincoln and proceeded to describe the whole affair in detail. St. Helen recovered, however, and left town, supposedly for Oklahoma. Bates, who spent years investigating the 🐾

claim, tried to bring the incident to the attention of the U.S. War Department, but he was dismissed.

AFTERMATH

Since then, more than a handful of theorists have concluded that it's plausible, if not entirely likely, that John Wilkes Booth actually escaped following the assassination of America's sixteenth president. Many believe Booth was involved in a conspiracy with the U.S. government to have Lincoln killed and was allowed, even helped, by the military to make his getaway. The man who was killed that night in the Virginia barn was either a patsy or someone simply shot by mistake. Oddly enough, there have been some clues, although yet unsubstantiated, that Boston Corbett, the man credited as Booth's killer, also lived out his final days in Enid, which raises some interesting questions about a possible association between him and David George. In recent years, a group of researchers, joined by several members of the surviving Booth family, petitioned to disinter the man buried in John Wilkes Booth's unmarked plot in Maryland to prove whether or not he's really the man he's supposed to be. Unfortunately, their request was denied. So, the mystery, at least to many, is still unsolved.

As for David George's mummy, Finis Bates acquired it from the funeral parlor in Enid and toured the country with it, putting it on display and renting it out to carnivals. It even made an appearance at the 1904 St. Louis World's Fair. Following Bates's death, the mummy changed hands several times and was eventually lost.

The hotel in which David George made his confession, however, still stands in Enid. Today it's the site of Garfield Furniture.

✸ **Garfield Furniture, 205 S. Grand Ave.,**
Enid, OK 73701, (580) 237-5032,
www.garfieldfurniture.com

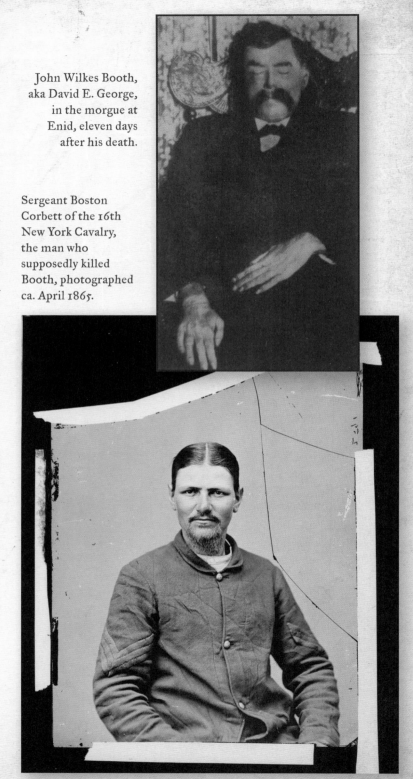

John Wilkes Booth, aka David E. George, in the morgue at Enid, eleven days after his death.

Sergeant Boston Corbett of the 16th New York Cavalry, the man who supposedly killed Booth, photographed ca. April 1865.

CONFEDERATE GHOST

The Thompson Island Bridge in San Marcos, TX, is said to be haunted by the ghost of a long-dead Confederate soldier. He died there at his post while guarding it during the Civil War. It is believed that he still appears there, dressed in his gray-and-yellow uniform, cap, and cape and armed with a Kentucky muzzleloader rifle. Although sightings are infrequent, the dead soldier's ghost seems to be more active before and during wartime.

His ghost has been reported walking near the bridge since the 1920s. In 1939, two men fixing a flat tire on the bridge were startled by the figure of a tall man wearing a rebel cap. Because the man was carrying a rifle, one of the two businessmen went for a gun in the car, but the apparition disappeared before he could confront it. Legend says the ghost is a man who lived in a cabin near the bridge before the Civil War. When he and his brother went off to fight for the South, they promised each other that they would return home, no matter what happened.

— *Tim Stevens*

✵ **Thompson Island Bridge is located over the San Marcos River on the road between San Marcos and Nixon, TX.**

A Confederate soldier from Texas carrying a Kentucky muzzleloader rifle, ca. 1864.

DEAD MAN'S HOLE

The world is full of so-called Dead Man's Holes—treacherous natural fissures in the landscape that can snare a careless hiker. Some appear to have a history of actual dead men, while others may be so nicknamed just to intrigue tourists.

In Texas alone, there are no fewer than four Dead Man's Holes. Three aren't exactly holes, just hollows of some kind, and there are no known stories involving the deceased. The name just sounded good to someone. Number four, however, meets the sinister title's criteria in full: It's a hole, and it has had a dead man in it—several, in fact.

This place, located a few miles west of Austin, TX, just south of Marble Falls, has been known about for nearly two hundred years. It was discovered in 1821, when an entomologist, while studying nocturnal insects, was lucky enough not to fall in, and personally gave the chasm its new name. But the hole wouldn't earn its dismal moniker for a few more decades. It was during the Civil War, when Americans were pitted against one another, that people began throwing their enemies into the pit. Staunch Confederates, apparently looking to sway the vote for secession, murdered Union sympathizers and dumped the bodies down the hole. Legend has it that the limb of an oak tree that once shaded the opening was scarred by the weight of a noose—part of an all-in-one "human disposal."

Years later, those brave enough to descend into Dead Man's Hole began bringing up the bodies—or what was left of them. In all, the remains of seventeen men were recovered. Only three, however, were officially identified: a settler named Adolph Hoppe, who opposed the war; Judge John R. Scott, the first chief justice of Burnet County and a pro-Union voter; and Ben McKeever, who had had a run-in with local freedmen soon after the war. Some of the others were believed to be carpetbaggers who had simply disappeared in the night.

Further exploration of the cave wouldn't take place for several more years. Dead Man's Hole is apparently a gas fissure, fumes from which prevented anyone from spelunking very far. Finally, though, the geological orifice was thoroughly mapped and measured in 1968, when cavers recorded its depth at one hundred and fifty-five feet and discovered two branches—one that stretched an additional fifteen feet and a second that extended another thirty feet. Today, the hole's seven-foot aperture has been sealed off, with only a small, barred entryway to allow anyone a look-see. And the only things you'll see down there nowadays are bottles, cans, and maybe a few coins. A caver did, however, once unearth a stolen wallet, with a driver's license that had expired five years earlier.

Unfortunately, it's hard to tell just how deep Dead Man's Hole is, but if you drop a rock in just the right spot, you can hear it tumble for several seconds. Try not to sink too many down there, lest we collectively turn it into Dead Man's Indentation.

✳ **Dead Man's Hole is located on private property.**

☛ **"It was during the Civil War, when Americans were pitted against one another, that people began throwing their enemies into the pit."**

The plaque erected at the site of Dead Man's Hole near Marble Falls, TX.

DEAD MAN'S HOLE

A view of the hole, now covered by a grate.

HOSPITAL RETURNS FROM THE DEAD

The old Jefferson Davis Hospital in Houston was one of Texas's most legendary abandoned places. Immense, historic, and incredibly creepy, with a foundation literally built right on top of an old cemetery, this bastion of abandoned spookiness sat vacant for over twenty years behind its razor-sharp, wire-topped fence, a beacon to the bravest of urban explorers and ghost hunters.

But all of that ended, and not the way most people assumed it would. After a 2003 incident in which a group of teenage explorers were robbed at gunpoint by some criminals while inside the old hospital, the city fathers decided to tear down the place. But a coalition of volunteers came together to save and renovate the historic old building. It was converted into artists' lofts, and construction was completed in 2005. That's right—people live there! And given the history of this place, one can only imagine what they encounter late at night while supposedly in the privacy of their bedrooms.

The Jeff Davis Hospital originally opened in 1924 and was the first city-owned hospital that accepted indigent patients. It was built on land donated to the city by Houston's founders. What the founders didn't know is that the land actually happened to be a cemetery from the 1800s, filled with the remains of Houstonians from all walks of life: former slaves, Civil War veterans, victims of the yellow fever and cholera epidemics, and city aldermen. Whether or not the bodies were disinterred and moved is a matter of debate; it seems that no one is sure. But until the 1980s, some of

> "The land actually happened to be a cemetery from the 1800s, filled with the remains of Houstonians from all walks of life: former slaves, Civil War veterans, victims of the yellow fever and cholera epidemics, and city aldermen."

the graves on the grounds were still marked, and bones were still being unearthed during various constructions on adjacent lots. So it seems possible that the hospital still sits atop the final resting places of many Houstonians.

There are those who believe that the angry spirits of these disrupted dead made their presence known from Jeff Davis's start. The hospital always seemed to have a higher-than-usual occurrence of strange encounters, apparitions, and anomalies. Many patients, visitors, and even hospital employees reportedly saw eerie figures in the hallways and heard the crying of disembodied voices. Even years after the hospital was no longer in use and sat neglected and empty, rumors of hauntings and strange happenings persisted. Some say that the many patients who died there only added to the ghostly population. Often, those who were brave enough to explore its dark and rotting halls claimed to have felt watchful eyes on them or to have heard or seen some of the various spectral figures said to haunt the hospital.

Seekers of the weird may be disappointed that the old Jeff Davis of urban-exploration legend—with its many jagged, broken windows and halls filled with darkness—is gone. But it's cool to know that rather than being demolished, this spooky old treasure was preserved.

✵ **The Jefferson Davis Hospital was converted into private apartments.**

A photographs of the old Jefferson Davis Hospital in a state of ruin, before it was renovated.

CONTRIBUTORS

From *Weird Maryland*, by Matt Lake;
© 2007 by Mark Sceurman and Mark Moran
The Ghost of Big Liz: 92
More Macabre Medicine: 94–95
Old Soldiers Never Die. Likewise, Airmen and Sailors: 96
Gathland Park's Spook Hill: 98
The Green Arm of Antietam: 111
Other contributors:
The Big Liz Revolution: 93l, Brendan
Summoning Big Liz: 93r, Shelley
Lookout: It's Smallpox: 97t, Sean Myers
It Wasn't Me!?: 97b, thestereogod
Spook Hill's Hoofprints of Gravity: 99t, Anonymous
Brother Against Brother in Finzel Cemetery: 99b,
    Beverly Litsinger, MarylandGhosts.zoomshare.com
Cedar Hill Cemetery: Lost and Found: 100–101,
    Brian Goodman
Antietam Days with Dad: 111r, Les

From *Weird Missouri*, by James Strait;
© 2008 by Mark Sceurman and Mark Moran
Unmarked Madam: 166

From *Weird Ohio*, by James A. Willis,
Andrew Henderson, and Loren Coleman;
© 2005 by Mark Sceurman and Mark Moran
No Retreat for Confederate Soldier: 170–71

From *Weird Oklahoma*, by Wesley Treat;
© 2011 by Mark Sceurman and Mark Moran
The Secret Life of John Wilkes Booth: 192–94
The Tri-State Spook Light: 188–90
Other contributor:
Spook Light Spotting Is a Family Affair: 191, Nick Beef

From *Weird Pennsylvania*, by Matt Lake;
© 2005 by Mark Sceurman and Mark Moran
The Many Ghosts of Fort Mifflin: 116
Gettysburg Phantoms (The Great Ghosts of Gettysburg):
    118
Other contributors:
The Lincoln Flag: 114–15, Dr. Seymour O'Life
Ghostly Reenactor: 117, Ray Morgenweck

From *Weird Tennessee*, by Roger Manley;
© 2010 by Mark Sceurman and Mark Moran
Still Standing Watch at Fort Donelson: 44–45
Thunder Hole: 47
Old Green Eyes (or Yellow Eyes): 48–49
Minié Ball Miracle: 49r
The Petrified Soldier: 52–53
Officer's Gate Post: 54
Nathan Bedford Forrest: 55
Redrum in the Read Room: 56–57
The Great Locomotive Chase: 58–59
Sinking of the *Sultana*: 62–64
The Dashing Assassin's Mummy: 65–67
De Soto Was Here: 68
Perpetual Motion of Jackson's Wheel: 69
Cannonball Church: 70
Little Lil: 71
Other contributors:
Captain Jack's Revenge: 50–51, thanks to Chris
    and Bettie Card
Beautiful Jim Key: 60–61, thanks to Mim Eichler Rivas

From *Weird Texas*, by Wesley Treat,
Heather Shade, and Rob Riggs;
© 2005 by Mark Sceurman and Mark Moran
Dead Man's Hole: 196–97
Hospital Returns from the Dead: 198–99
Other contributor:
Confederate Ghost: 195, Tim Stevens

From *Weird Virginia*, by Jeff Bahr,
Troy Taylor, and Loren Coleman;
© 2007 by Mark Sceurman and Mark Moran
In Spirits of the Shenandoah Valley: 126–28
Phantom Stage: 128–29
The Gray Man of Waverly Farm: 130–31
Virginia Battlefield Ghost: 132–33
Lingering Ghosts of Kalorama: 134–35
Logan Still Looking for His Horse: 135r
The Ghost of Honest Abe: 136–37
The Hauntings of Jefferson Davis: 138–39
Hollywood Cemetery: 140
The Tombstone House: 142
Strong (Buried) Arm of the Confederacy: 143–45

INDEX

Note: Page numbers in **bold** indicate references to photo captions.

PICTURE CREDITS

ABOUT THE AUTHORS

MARK MORAN is a lifelong resident of New Jersey. After graduating from Parsons School of Design in 1983, he set out on a journey of weird discovery, wandering the back roads, back alleys, and backwoods of the U.S., listening to the tall tales locals would tell and photographing the unusual sites he found along the way. This odd quest would lead him to his unforeseen and unexpected roles as magazine publisher, author, and TV show host.

These days Mark lives a seemingly normal life in a quiet Jersey suburb with his wife and two daughters. Though his mild-mannered neighbors would never suspect it, each morning as he jumps into his Jeep to go to work, Mark begins a brand-new adventure into the unknown, seldom-explored, and all-but-forgotten side of American culture.

MARK SCEURMAN blended his love for New Jersey and his affection for the strange into a magazine called *Weird N.J.*, which explored every unbelievable tale he would hear while traveling around the state. The response to the publication was overwhelming, and the journey to uncover little-known weird stories about the other forty-nine states began. Mark has been in the publishing industry most of his life as a graphic designer, writer, and man behind-the-scenes on the New Jersey music front. He travels across the country—sometimes just jumps into the car and hits the road, with only cryptic notes and crude directions as guides. Currently, Mark lives in New Jersey with his wife, Shirley, and their daughter. He likes rock 'n' roll and vacations "down the shore," and was voted "most likely to spontaneously combust" in his high school yearbook.